a cook's book
of baking

BUTTER
SUGAR
FLOUR

MURDOCH BOOKS

Published by Murdoch Books Pty Limited.
www.murdochbooks.com.au

Murdoch Books Australia	Murdoch Books UK Limited
Pier 8/9, 23 Hickson Road	Erico House, 6th Floor North
Millers Point NSW 2000	93–99 Upper Richmond Road
Phone: + 61 (0) 2 8220 2000	Putney, London SW15 2TG
Fax: + 61 (0) 2 8220 2558	Phone: + 44 (0) 20 8785 5995
	Fax: + 44 (0) 20 8785 5985

Chief Executive: Juliet Rogers
Publisher: Kay Scarlett

Design Manager: Vivien Valk
Design Concept, Design and Illustration: Alex Frampton
Project Manager: Jacqueline Blanchard
Editor: Jan Hutchison
Introduction Text: Jan Hutchison
Recipes developed by the Murdoch Books Test Kitchen
Production: Monika Paratore

National Library of Australia Cataloguing-in-Publication Data
Butter, Sugar, Flour: a cook's book of baking. Includes index.
ISBN 978 1 74045 862 7. ISBN 1 74045 862 1.
1. Bakery. 2. Baked products. I. Title. 641.815

Printed by Midas Printing (Asia) Ltd. PRINTED IN CHINA.

IMPORTANT: Those who might be at risk from the effects of salmonella poisoning (the elderly, pregnant women, young children and those suffering from immune deficiency diseases) should consult their doctor with any concerns about eating raw eggs.

CONVERSION GUIDE: You may find cooking times vary depending on the oven you are using. For fan-forced ovens, as a general rule, set the oven temperature to 20°C (35°F) lower than indicated in the recipe. We have used 20 ml (4 teaspoon) tablespoon measures. If you are using a 15 ml (3 teaspoon) tablespoon, for most recipes the difference will not be noticeable. However, for recipes using baking powder, gelatine, bicarbonate of soda (baking soda), small amounts of flour, add an extra teaspoon for each tablespoon specified.

a cook's book
of baking

BUTTER
SUGAR
FLOUR

Contents

a host of baked goodies

There is nothing quite as comforting, or irresistible, as the delicious smells of home baking—the rewards of taking a tray of freshly cooked delights from the oven are many. Whoever first came up with the idea of combining these three essentially simple ingredients—butter, sugar and flour—to make batters and doughs, was onto a very good thing.

In this book you will find old recipes from granny's day alongside refreshing takes on all-time favourites and fabulous contemporary recipes, which are bound to be passed from one generation to another. Some are purely indulgent—making the most of such luscious ingredients as cream and chocolate, fresh dates and burstingly ripe berries. The ingredients in others—oats, seeds, semolina, dried fruits and nuts—are healthy enough to make them ideal for wholesome snacks or nutritious lunch box additions. Some are so simple they'll be a cinch to make with the kids, while others may be a little more time-consuming, and take a bit more of your patience and concentration—but the impression they will leave on your guests will be well worth your efforts.

There should be something for all tastes in this book. But it could be difficult deciding between making your own breakfast croissants, or taking on the culinary adventure of turning out Scottish baps or lavash for lunch. You can opt for the decadence of those delicious perennials—chocolate mud cake or black forest cake, or turn out a batch of comparatively understated yet no less scrumptious pistachio friands. Will you choose the lightness of a classic sponge for afternoon tea or the rich indulgence of a fig and raspberry cake, which could easily double as a dessert? When it comes to filling the cookie barrel, there's a tantalizing range from traditional melting moments to florentines and mouth-watering Viennese fingers. Sometimes only a slice will suffice—macadamia blondies or sticky toffee slice perhaps? And you will no longer need to head to your nearest café if you have a sudden urge for Portuguese custard tarts, lemon meringue pie, baklava or tarte tatin—all your baking ideas are right here.

In short, baking is back. And the range and quality of kitchen equipment now available makes the once arduous tasks of beating, whipping and kneading a breeze. Buy the best quality ingredients you can afford, borrow baking pans and beaters if you need to, and make a beeline for the kitchen!

brioche hot cross buns croissants chelsea buns

Breads and buns

es pumpernickel baguettes cottage loaf stollen

Baguettes

Makes 3 loaves

2 teaspoons (7 g/¼ oz) dried yeast
1 teaspoon sugar
90 g (3¼ oz/¾ cup) plain (all-purpose) flour
375 g (13 oz/3 cups) strong flour
2 tablespoons polenta, to sprinkle

1 Place the yeast, sugar and 310 ml (10¾ fl oz/1¼ cups) warm water in a small bowl and mix well. Leave in a warm place for 10 minutes, or until bubbles appear on the surface. The mixture should be frothy and slightly increased in volume.

2 Mix together the flours and ½ teaspoon salt and transfer half the dry ingredients to a large bowl. Make a well in the centre and add the yeast mixture. Using a large metal spoon, fold the remaining flour into the yeast mixture. This should form a soft dough. Cover the bowl with a damp tea (dish) towel or plastic wrap and set aside for 30–35 minutes, or until frothy and risen by about one-third of its original size.

3 Mix in the remaining dry ingredients and add up to 60 ml (2 fl oz/ ¼ cup) warm water, enough to form a soft but slightly sticky dough. Knead the dough on a lightly floured surface for about 10 minutes, until smooth and elastic. If the dough sticks to the work surface while kneading, flour the surface sparingly, but try to avoid adding too much flour.

4 Shape the dough into a ball and place in a large, lightly greased bowl. Cover with a damp tea towel or plastic wrap and leave in a warm place for about 1 hour, or until the dough has doubled in size.

5 Lightly grease two large baking trays and sprinkle with polenta. Punch down the dough and knead for 2–3 minutes. Divide the dough into three portions and press or roll each into a rectangle about 20 x 40 cm (8 x 16 inches). Roll each up firmly into a long sausage shape and place, seam side down, well spaced on the prepared trays. Cover loosely with a damp tea towel or plastic wrap and set aside in a warm place for 40 minutes, or until doubled in size.

6 Preheat the oven to 220°C (425°F/Gas 7). Lightly brush the loaves with water and make diagonal slashes across the top at 6 cm (2½ inch) intervals using a sharp knife.

7 Bake for 20 minutes, then lower the temperature to 180°C (350°F/Gas 4) and bake for another 5–10 minutes, or until the crust is golden and firm and the base sounds hollow when tapped underneath. Cool on a wire rack.

Baguettes are best eaten within a few hours of baking.

Cottage Loaf

Makes 1 large loaf

2 teaspoons (7 g/^{1}/4 oz) dried yeast
1 tablespoon soft brown sugar
250 g (9 oz/1^2/3 cups) strong flour
300 g (10^1/2 oz/2 cups) wholemeal (whole-wheat) flour
1 tablespoon vegetable oil

1   Place the yeast, 1 teaspoon of the sugar and 125 ml (4 fl oz/^{1}/2 cup) warm water in a small bowl and mix well. Leave in a warm, draught-free place for 10 minutes, or until bubbles appear on the surface. The mixture should be frothy and slightly increased in volume.

2   Place the flours and 1 teaspoon salt in a large bowl. Make a well in the centre and add the yeast mixture, oil, remaining sugar and 250 ml (9 fl oz/1 cup) warm water. Mix with a wooden spoon, then turn out onto a lightly floured surface. Knead for 10 minutes, or until smooth and elastic. Incorporate a little extra flour into the dough as you knead, to stop the dough from sticking.

3   Place the dough in an oiled bowl and lightly brush oil over the dough. Cover with plastic wrap or a damp tea (dish) towel and leave in a warm place for 45 minutes, or until doubled in size.

4   Punch down the dough, then turn out onto a lightly floured surface and knead for 3–4 minutes. Pull away one-third of the dough and knead both portions into smooth balls. Place the large ball on a large floured baking tray and brush the top with water. Sit the smaller ball on top and, using two fingers, press down into the centre of the dough to join the two balls together. Cover with plastic wrap or a damp tea towel and set aside in a warm place for 40 minutes, or until well risen.

5 Preheat the oven to 190°C (375°F/Gas 5). Sift some white flour over the top of the loaf and bake for 40 minutes, or until golden brown and cooked. Leave on the tray for 2–3 minutes to cool slightly, then turn out onto a wire rack to cool.

 This is a traditional English style of bread with a distinctive look. It can be made with both white or wholemeal (whole-wheat) flours or a combination of the two. It can be formed into any shape you like, either free-form or cooked in a bread tin.

Brioche

Makes 6 small and 1 medium brioche

2 teaspoons (7 g/¹/4 oz) dried yeast
1 teaspoon caster (superfine) sugar
125 ml (4 fl oz/¹/2 cup) warm milk
530 g (1 lb 2 oz/4¹/4 cups) plain (all-purpose) flour
2 tablespoons caster (superfine) sugar, extra
4 eggs, at room temperature, lightly beaten
175 g (6 oz) butter, softened
1 egg yolk, extra
1 tablespoon pouring (whipping) cream

1   Grease six small brioche moulds and a 21 x 11 cm (8¹/4 x 4¹/4 inch)
    bread or loaf (bar) tin.

2   Place the yeast, sugar and warm milk in a small bowl and stir well.
    Leave in a warm, draught-free place for 10 minutes, or until bubbles
    appear on the surface. The mixture should be frothy and slightly
    increased in volume.

3   Sift 500 g (l lb 2 oz/4 cups) of the flour, 1 teaspoon salt and the
    extra sugar into a large bowl. Make a well in the centre and pour in the
    yeast mixture and beaten eggs. Beat the mixture with a wooden spoon
    until well combined and the mixture forms a rough ball.

4   Turn out onto a lightly floured surface and knead for 5 minutes,
    or until the dough is smooth and firm. Gradually incorporate
    small amounts of the butter into the dough. This will take about
    10 minutes and the dough will be very sticky.

5   Sprinkle a clean work surface, your hands and the dough with a
    small amount of the remaining flour. Knead the dough lightly for

10 minutes, or until smooth and elastic. Place in a large, buttered bowl and brush the surface with oil. Cover with plastic wrap and leave in a warm place for 1½–2 hours, or until well risen.

6 Punch down the dough and divide in half. Cover one half with plastic wrap and set aside. Divide the other half into six even-sized pieces. Remove a quarter of the dough from each piece. Mould the larger pieces into even rounds and place into the brioche moulds. Brush the surface with the glaze made by combining the extra egg yolk and cream. Shape the small pieces into small even-sized balls and place on top of each roll. Push a floured wooden skewer through the centre of the top ball to the base of the roll, then remove—this will secure the ball to the roll. Brush again with the glaze, cover and leave in a warm place for 45 minutes, or until well risen. Meanwhile, place the remaining dough in the prepared tin and brush with glaze. Cover and set aside for 1 hour, or until well risen.

7 Preheat the oven to 210°C (415°F/Gas 6–7). Bake the small brioche for 10 minutes. Reduce the oven temperature to 180°C (350°F/Gas 4) and bake for 10 minutes, or until golden and cooked. Turn out immediately onto a wire rack to cool.

8 Increase the oven to 210°C (415°F/Gas 6–7). Bake the medium loaf for 15 minutes. Reduce the oven temperature to 180°C (350°F/Gas 4) and bake for 15 minutes, or until golden and cooked. Turn out onto a wire rack to cool.

 If the brioche moulds are not available you can bake the dough as two loaves.

English Muffins

Makes 15

2 teaspooons (7 g/¼ oz) dried yeast
½ teaspoon sugar
530 g (1 lb 2 oz/4¼ cups) plain (all-purpose) flour
350 ml (12 fl oz) lukewarm milk
1 egg, lightly beaten
40 g (1½ oz) butter, melted

1   Lightly dust two 32 x 28 cm (12¾ x 11¼ inch) baking trays
    with flour. Put the yeast, sugar, 1 teaspoon of the flour and 60 ml
    (2 fl oz/¼ cup) warm water in a small bowl and mix well. Leave in a
    warm place for 10 minutes, or until bubbles appear on the surface.
    The mixture should be frothy and slightly increased in volume.

2   Sift the remaining flour and 1 teaspoon salt into a large bowl. Make a
    well in the centre and add the milk, egg, butter and yeast mixture all
    at once. Using a flat-bladed knife, mix to a soft dough.

3   Turn the dough out onto a lightly floured surface and knead lightly
    for 2 minutes, or until smooth. Shape the dough into a ball and place
    in a large, lightly oiled bowl. Cover with plastic wrap or a damp tea
    (dish) towel and leave in a warm place for 1½ hours, or until well risen.

4   Preheat the oven to 210°C (415°F/Gas 6–7). Punch down the dough
    and knead again for 2 minutes, or until smooth. Roll to 1 cm (½ inch)
    thick, then cut into rounds with a lightly floured plain 8 cm (3¼ inch)
    cutter and place on the trays. Cover with plastic wrap or a damp tea
    (dish) towel and leave in a warm, draught-free place for 10 minutes.

5   Bake for 15 minutes, turning once halfway through cooking. Transfer
    to a wire rack to cool. Serve warm or cold.

Banana Bread

Makes 1 loaf

250 g (9 oz/2 cups) plain (all-purpose) flour
2 teaspoons baking powder
1 teaspoon mixed (pumpkin pie) spice
150 g (5¹/₂ oz) unsalted butter, softened
185 g (6¹/₂ oz/1 cup) soft brown sugar
2 eggs, lightly beaten
240 g (8¹/₂ oz/1 cup) mashed ripe bananas (about 2 bananas)

1. Preheat the oven to 180°C (350°F/Gas 4). Grease and line the base of a 23 x 13 x 6 cm (9 x 5 x 2¹/₂ inch) loaf (bar) tin.

2. Sift together the flour, baking powder, mixed spice and ¹/₄ teaspoon salt into a bowl.

3. Cream the butter and sugar in a large bowl with electric beaters until light and fluffy. Add the eggs gradually, beating well after each addition, and beat until smooth. Mix in the banana. Gradually add the sifted dry ingredients and mix until smooth.

4. Pour into the loaf tin and bake on the middle shelf of the oven for 35–45 minutes, or until the top is golden brown and a skewer inserted into the centre comes out clean. Cool in the tin for 10 minutes before turning out onto a wire rack.

This bread is delicious eaten warm. It will keep for a few days wrapped in plastic wrap. The flavour improves on keeping. It can also be toasted.

Swedish Tea Ring

Makes 1

2 teaspoons (7 g/^{1}/$_4$ oz) dried yeast
170 ml (5^1/$_2$ fl oz/^{2}/$_3$ cup) milk
60 g (2^1/$_4$ oz) unsalted butter, softened
2 tablespoons caster (superfine) sugar
375 g (13 oz/3 cups) plain (all-purpose) flour
1 egg, lightly beaten
1 egg yolk, extra

FILLING
30 g (1 oz) unsalted butter
1 tablespoon caster (superfine) sugar
100 g (3^1/$_2$ oz/^{2}/$_3$ cup) coarsely ground blanched almonds
95 g (3^1/$_4$ oz/^{1}/$_2$ cup) mixed dried fruit
100 g (3^1/$_2$ oz/^{1}/$_2$ cup) glacé (candied) cherries, cut in half

ICING
125 g (4^1/$_2$ oz/1 cup) icing (confectioners') sugar
1–2 tablespoons milk
2 drops natural almond extract

1 Lightly grease a baking tray or line with baking paper. Dissolve the yeast in 2 tablespoons warm water in a bowl and leave in a warm place for 10 minutes, or until bubbles appear on the surface. Heat the milk, butter, sugar and ^{1}/$_2$ teaspoon salt in a saucepan until just warmed.

2 Sift 250 g (9 oz/2 cups) of the flour into a large bowl. Add the yeast and milk mixtures and beaten egg and mix to a smooth batter. Add enough of the remaining flour to make a soft dough. Turn out onto a

lightly floured surface and knead for 10 minutes, or until the dough is smooth and elastic. Place the dough in a large, lightly oiled bowl and brush the dough with oil. Cover with plastic wrap or a damp tea (dish) towel and leave in a warm place for 1 hour, or until well risen.

3 Meanwhile, to make the filling, cream the butter and sugar, then mix in the almonds, mixed fruit and glacé cherries.

4 Punch down the dough and knead for 1 minute. Roll the dough to a 25 x 45 cm (10 x 18 inch) rectangle. Spread the filling over the dough, leaving a 2 cm (3/4 inch) border. Roll up and form into a ring with the seam underneath. Mix the egg yolk with 1 tablespoon water and use a little to seal the ends together.

5 Place the tea ring on the prepared baking tray. Snip with scissors from the outside edge at 4 cm (1 1/2 inch) intervals. Turn the cut pieces on the side and flatten slightly. Cover with plastic wrap and leave in a warm place for 45 minutes, or until well risen.

6 Preheat the oven to 180°C (350°F/Gas 4). Brush the tea ring with some of the egg yolk and water mixture and bake for 20–25 minutes, or until firm and golden. Cover with foil if the tea cake is browning too much. Remove and cool.

7 To make the icing, combine the icing sugar, milk and almond extract until smooth. Drizzle over the tea ring.

 This tea ring will keep for 3 days in an airtight container. It will freeze, un-iced, for 1 month.

Finger Buns

Makes 12

500 g (1 lb 2 oz/4 cups) plain (all-purpose) flour
35 g (1¼ oz/⅓ cup) full-cream powdered milk
4 teaspoons (14 g/½ oz) dried yeast
125 g (4½ oz/½ cup) caster (superfine) sugar
80 g (2¾ oz/⅔ cup) sultanas (golden raisins)
60 g (2¼ oz) unsalted butter, melted
1 egg, lightly beaten
1 egg yolk, extra

ICING
155 g (5½ oz/1¼ cups) icing (confectioners') sugar
20 g (¾ oz) unsalted butter, melted
pink food colouring

1   Mix 375 g (13 oz/3 cups) of the flour with the milk powder, yeast, sugar, sultanas and ½ teaspoon salt in a large bowl. Make a well in the centre.

2   Combine the butter, egg and 250 ml (9 fl oz/1 cup) warm water and add all at once to the flour. Stir for 2 minutes, or until well combined. Add enough of the remaining flour to make a soft dough.

3   Turn out onto a lightly floured surface. Knead for 10 minutes, or until the dough is smooth and elastic, adding more flour if necessary. Place in a large, lightly oiled bowl and brush with oil. Cover with plastic wrap and leave in a warm place for 1 hour, or until well risen.

4   Lightly grease two large baking trays. Preheat the oven to 180°C (350°F/Gas 4). Punch down the dough and knead for 1 minute.

Divide into 12 portions. Shape each into a 15 cm (6 inch) long oval. Put on the trays 5 cm (2 inches) apart. Cover with plastic wrap and set aside in a warm place for 20–25 minutes, or until well risen.

5 Mix the extra egg yolk with 1½ teaspoons water and brush over the dough. Bake for 12–15 minutes, or until firm and golden. Transfer to a wire rack to cool.

6 To make the icing, stir the icing sugar, melted butter and 2–3 teaspoons water together in a bowl until smooth. Mix in a little food colouring and spread over the tops of the buns.

Pumpernickel

Makes 2 loaves

4 teaspoons (14 g/$^1/_2$ oz) dried yeast
1 teaspoon caster (superfine) sugar
90 g (3$^1/_4$ oz/$^1/_4$ cup) molasses
60 ml (2 fl oz/$^1/_4$ cup) cider vinegar
90 g (3$^1/_4$ oz) butter
30 g (1 oz/$^1/_4$ cup) chopped dark chocolate
1 tablespoon instant coffee powder
560 g (1 lb 4 oz/4$^1/_2$ cups) plain (all-purpose) flour
300 g (10$^1/_2$ oz/3 cups) rye flour
75 g (2$^1/_2$ oz/1 cup) unprocessed bran
1 tablespoon caraway seeds
2 teaspoons fennel seeds
1 egg white
caraway seeds, extra

1 Grease a 20 cm (8 inch) round cake tin and a 28 x 12 cm (11$^1/_4$ x 4$^1/_2$ inch) loaf (bar) or bread tin, or use any baking tin that has a 1.75 litre (61 fl oz) capacity. Line the base of each tin with baking paper.

2 Put 125 ml (4 fl oz/$^1/_2$ cup) warm water, the yeast and sugar in a small bowl and stir well. Leave in a warm, draught-free place for 10 minutes, or until bubbles appear on the surface. The mixture should be frothy and slightly increased in volume.

3 Put the molasses, vinegar, butter, chocolate, coffee powder and 500 ml (17 fl oz/2 cups) cold water into a saucepan and stir over low heat until the butter and chocolate have melted and the mixture is just warmed.

4 Place 435 g (15¼ oz/3½ cups) of the plain flour, the rye flour, bran, caraway and fennel seeds and 1 teaspoon salt in a large bowl. Make a well in the centre and add the yeast and chocolate mixtures. Using a wooden spoon, and then your hands, combine the dough until it leaves the side of the bowl and forms a firm, sticky ball.

5 Turn out onto a heavily floured surface and knead for 10 minutes. Incorporate enough of the remaining plain flour to make a dense but smooth and elastic dough. Divide in half and place in separate lightly oiled bowls. Brush the surface of the dough with melted butter or oil. Cover with plastic wrap or a damp tea (dish) towel and leave in a warm, draught-free place for 1¼ hours, or until well risen. Punch down the dough and knead each for 1 minute. Shape each portion to fit a tin and place one portion in each tin. Cover with lightly oiled plastic wrap or a damp tea towel and leave in a warm place for 1 hour, or until well risen.

6 Preheat the oven to 180°C (350°F/Gas 4). Glaze the dough with the combined egg white and 1 tablespoon water and sprinkle with extra caraway seeds. Bake for 50 minutes, or until well browned. During the last 15 minutes, cover with foil to prevent excessive browning. Leave in the tins for 15 minutes before turning out onto a wire rack to cool.

Pumpernickel is a dense rye bread that originated in Germany. It is delicious with soft cheeses, olives, smoked salmon and dill pickles.

Chelsea Buns

Makes 8

2 teaspoons (7 g/^{1}/$_4$ oz) dried yeast

1 teaspoon sugar

310 g (11 oz/2^1/$_2$ cups) plain (all-purpose) flour, sifted

125 ml (4 fl oz/^{1}/$_2$ cup) warm milk

185 g (6^1/$_2$ oz) unsalted butter, cubed

1 tablespoon sugar, extra

2 teaspoons grated lemon zest

1 teaspoon mixed (pumpkin pie) spice

1 egg, lightly beaten

45 g (1^1/$_2$ oz/^{1}/$_4$ cup) soft brown sugar

185 g (6^1/$_2$ oz/1 cup) mixed dried fruit

1 tablespoon milk, extra, to glaze

2 tablespoons sugar, extra, to glaze

ICING
60 g (2^1/$_4$ oz/^{1}/$_2$ cup) icing (confectioners') sugar

1–2 tablespoons milk

1 Combine the yeast, sugar and 1 tablespoon of the flour in a small bowl. Add the milk and mix until smooth. Set aside in a warm place for 10 minutes, or until bubbles appear on the surface.

2 Place the remaining flour in a large bowl and rub in 125 g (4^1/$_2$ oz) of the butter with your fingertips. Stir in the extra sugar, lemon zest and half the mixed spice. Make a well, add the yeast mixture and egg and mix. Gather together and turn out onto a lightly floured surface.

3 Knead for 2 minutes, or until smooth, then shape into a ball. Place in a large, lightly oiled bowl, cover with plastic wrap and set aside in a warm place for 1 hour, or until well risen. Punch down the dough and knead for 2 minutes, or until smooth.

4 Preheat the oven to 210°C (415°F/Gas 6–7). Lightly grease a baking tray.

5 Cream the remaining butter with the brown sugar in a small bowl with electric beaters until light and fluffy. Roll the dough out to a 40 x 25 cm (16 x 10 inch) rectangle. Spread the butter mixture all over the dough to within 2 cm (3/4 inch) of the edge of one of the longer sides. Spread with the combined fruit and remaining mixed spice. Roll the dough from the long side, firmly and evenly, to enclose the fruit. Use a sharp knife to cut the roll into eight slices about 5 cm (2 inches) wide. Arrange the slices, close together and with the seams inwards, on the tray. Flatten slightly.

6 Set aside, covered with plastic wrap, in a warm place for 30 minutes, or until well risen. Bake for 20 minutes, or until brown and cooked. When almost ready, stir the extra milk and sugar in a small saucepan over low heat until the sugar dissolves and the mixture is almost boiling. Brush over the hot buns. Cool.

7 To make the icing, mix the icing sugar and milk, stir until smooth, then drizzle over the buns.

Croissants

Makes 12

350 ml (12 fl oz) warm milk
2 teaspoons (7 g / ¼ oz) dried yeast
60 g (2¼ oz / ¼ cup) caster (superfine) sugar
405 g (14¼ oz / 3¼ cups) plain (all-purpose) flour
250 g (9 oz) unsalted butter, at room temperature
1 egg

1 Combine the milk, yeast and 1 tablespoon of the sugar in a small bowl and stir until dissolved. Leave in a warm place for 10 minutes, or until bubbles appear on the surface. The mixture should be frothy and slightly increased in volume.

2 Place the flour, 1 teaspoon salt and remaining sugar in a large bowl and make a well in the centre. Pour the yeast mixture into the well and mix to a rough dough with a wooden spoon. Turn out onto a floured surface and knead for 10 minutes, or until smooth and elastic. Add only a small amount of flour—just enough to stop the dough sticking. Place in a greased large bowl, cover and set aside in a warm place for 1 hour, or until doubled in size.

3 Meanwhile, place the butter between two sheets of baking paper, cut in half lengthways and use a rolling pin to pat out to a 20 x 10 cm (8 x 4 inch) rectangle. Cover and refrigerate the butter.

4 Punch down the dough by hitting once to expel the air. Knead briefly on a lightly floured surface, then roll to a 45 x 12 cm (18 x 4½ inch) rectangle. Place the butter on the lower half of the dough and fold down the top half. Seal the edges using your fingertips.

5. Turn the folded side of the dough to the right. Roll out the dough to a rectangle about 45 x 22 cm (18 x 8½ inches), then fold up the bottom third and fold down the top third. Wrap in plastic wrap for 20 minutes.

6. Roll again with the fold to the right. Chill for 20 minutes, then repeat the process two more times. The butter should be completely incorporated—roll again if not incorporated.

7. Lightly brush two baking trays with melted butter. Cut the dough in half. Roll each half into a large rectangle and trim each to about 36 x 22 cm (14 x 8½ inches). Cut a cardboard triangular template 18 cm (7 inches) across the base and 14 cm (5½ inches) along each side. Cut each rectangle into six triangles. Stretch each triangle a little to extend its length. Roll each triangle into a crescent, starting from the base. Place well apart on the prepared trays, cover and refrigerate for a minimum of 4 hours, or overnight.

8. Lightly beat the egg with 2 teaspoons water in a small bowl. Brush the pastries with egg wash and set aside for 40 minutes, or until doubled in bulk. Preheat the oven to 200°C (400°F/Gas 6). Brush again with egg wash. Bake for 15–20 minutes, or until crisp and golden.

Beer Bread

Makes 1 loaf

405 g (14¹/4 oz/2³/4 cups) strong flour
3 teaspoons baking powder
1 tablespoon caster (superfine) sugar
2 teaspoons dill seeds
50 g (1³/4 oz) butter, chilled and cubed
375 ml (13 fl oz/1¹/2 cups) beer
plain (all-purpose) flour, to dust
dill seeds, extra
coarse sea salt

1   Preheat the oven to 210°C (415°F/Gas 6–7). Lightly grease a
    baking tray. Sift the flour, baking powder and 1 teaspoon salt
    into a large bowl.

2   Add the sugar and dill seeds and combine. Rub the butter into the
    dry ingredients using your fingertips, until the mixture resembles
    breadcrumbs. Make a well in the centre and add the beer all at once.
    Using a wooden spoon, quickly mix to form a soft dough.

3   Turn out onto a floured surface, sprinkling extra flour on your hands
    and on the surface of the dough. Knead for 1–2 minutes, or until the
    dough forms a smooth ball. Elongate the ball slightly, flatten a little,
    and with the blunt end of a large knife press down 2 cm (³/4 inch)
    along the centre. Brush the surface with water, and sprinkle liberally
    with the extra dill seeds and sea salt.

4   Bake for 20 minutes, then reduce the oven to 180°C (350°F/Gas 4) and
    bake for another 15–20 minutes, or until the bread sounds hollow when
    tapped. Remove from the oven, place on a wire rack and leave to cool.

Scottish Baps

Makes 12

2 teaspoons (7 g/¹/₄ oz) dried yeast
1 teaspoon caster (superfine) sugar
435 g (15¹/₄ oz/3 cups) strong flour
250 ml (9 fl oz/1 cup) lukewarm milk
45 g (1¹/₂ oz) butter, melted
1 tablespoon plain (all-purpose) flour, to dust

1 Lightly dust two baking trays with flour. Place the yeast, sugar and 2 tablespoons of the strong flour in a small bowl. Gradually add the milk, blending until smooth and dissolved. Leave in a warm, draught-free place for 10 minutes, or until bubbles appear on the surface. The mixture should be frothy and slightly increased in volume.

2 Sift the remaining strong flour and 1¹/₂ teaspoons salt into a large bowl. Make a well in the centre and add the yeast mixture and butter. Using a knife, mix to form a soft dough. Turn the dough onto a lightly floured surface and knead for 3 minutes, or until smooth. Shape into a ball and place in a large, oiled bowl. Cover with plastic wrap or a damp tea (dish) towel and leave in a warm place for 1 hour, or until well risen.

3 Preheat the oven to 210°C (415°F/Gas 6–7). Punch down the dough. Knead the dough for 2 minutes, or until smooth. Divide into 12 portions. Knead one portion at a time on a lightly floured surface, then shape into a flat oval. Repeat with the remaining dough.

4 Place the baps on the trays and dust with the plain flour. Cover with plastic wrap and leave in a warm place for 15 minutes, or until well risen. Make an indent in the centre of each oval with your finger. Bake for 30 minutes, or until browned and cooked through. Serve warm.

Light Fruit Bread

Makes 1 loaf

160 g (5³/4 oz/1¹/4 cups) raisins
1 tablespoon sherry
1 tablespoon grated orange zest
1 teaspoon dried yeast
250 ml (9 fl oz/1 cup) warm milk
60 g (2¹/4 oz/¹/4 cup) caster (superfine) sugar
375 g (13 oz/2¹/2 cups) strong flour
30 g (1 oz) butter, cubed

GLAZE
1 egg yolk
2 tablespoons pouring (whipping) cream

1 Combine the raisins, sherry and orange zest in a bowl and set aside.

2 Place the yeast, milk and 1 teaspoon of the sugar in a small bowl and mix well. Leave in a warm, draught-free place for 10 minutes, or until bubbles appear on the surface. The mixture should be frothy and slightly increased in volume.

3 Place 340 g (11³/4 oz/2¹/3 cups) of the flour and ¹/2 teaspoon salt in a large bowl. Rub in the butter and remaining sugar with your fingertips. Make a well in the centre, add the yeast mixture and mix to a soft dough.

4 Turn out onto a floured surface and knead for 10 minutes, or until smooth and elastic, incorporating the remaining flour as necessary.

5 Place the dough in an oiled bowl and brush with oil. Cover with plastic wrap or a damp tea (dish) towel and leave for 1 hour, or until

well risen. Punch down the dough, knead for 2 minutes, then roll to a rectangle, 40 x 20 cm (16 x 8 inches). Scatter with the raisin mixture and roll up firmly from the long end.

6 Grease a 21 x 8 cm (8¼ x 3¼ inch) loaf (bar) tin and line the base with baking paper. Place the dough in the tin, cover with plastic wrap or a damp tea (dish) towel and leave for 30 minutes, or until well risen. Preheat the oven to 180°C (350°F/Gas 4).

7 To make the glaze, combine the egg yolk and cream and brush a little over the loaf. Bake for 30 minutes, or until cooked and golden. Glaze again, bake for 5 minutes, then glaze again. Cool on a wire rack.

Sherry is a fortified wine made from white grapes. It can be sweet, medium or dry in flavour—in baking, sweet sherry is usually used.

Mini Wholemeal Loaves

Makes 4 small loaves

2 teaspoons (7 g/¼ oz) dried yeast
1 tablespoon caster (superfine) sugar
125 ml (4 fl oz/½ cup) warm milk
600 g (1 lb 5 oz/4 cups) wholemeal (whole-wheat) strong flour
60 ml (2 fl oz/¼ cup) oil
1 egg, lightly beaten

1 Grease four 13 x 6 x 5 cm (5 x 2½ x 2 inch) baking tins. Place the yeast, sugar and milk in a small bowl and mix well. Leave in a warm, draught-free place for 10 minutes, or until bubbles appear on the surface. The mixture should be frothy and slightly increased in volume.

2 Place the flour and 1 teaspoon salt in a large bowl, make a well in the centre and add the yeast mixture, oil and 250 ml (9 fl oz/1 cup) warm water. Mix to a soft dough and gather into a ball. Turn out onto a floured surface and knead for 10 minutes. Add a little extra flour if the dough is too sticky. Place the dough in a oiled bowl, cover loosely with plastic wrap or a damp tea (dish) towel and leave in a warm place for 1 hour, or until well risen.

3 Punch down the dough, turn out onto a floured surface and knead for 1 minute, or until smooth. Divide into four portions, knead into shape and put in the tins. Cover loosely with plastic wrap or a damp tea towel and leave in a warm place for 45 minutes, or until risen.

4 Preheat the oven to 210°C (415°F/Gas 6–7). Brush the loaves with the egg. Bake for 10 minutes, then reduce the oven temperature to 180°C (350°F/Gas 4) and bake for 30–35 minutes, or until the base sounds hollow when tapped. Cover with foil if the tops become too brown.

Pumpkin Scones

Makes 12

30 g (1 oz) butter, cubed
2 tablespoons caster (superfine) sugar
125 g (4½ oz/½ cup) mashed cooked pumpkin (winter squash)
1 egg, lightly beaten
125 ml (4 fl oz/½ cup) milk
310 g (11 oz/2½ cups) self-raising flour
milk, extra, to glaze

1 Preheat the oven to 210°C (415°F/Gas 6–7). Brush a baking tray with melted butter or oil.

2 Using electric beaters, beat the butter and sugar in a small bowl until light and creamy. Add the pumpkin, egg and milk and mix well.

3 Sift the flour and ½ teaspoon salt into a large bowl. Make a well in the centre and add almost all of the pumpkin mixture. Mix lightly with a flat-bladed knife to a soft dough, adding more liquid if necessary.

4 Knead the dough briefly on a lightly floured surface. Press or roll out the dough to 2 cm (¾ inch) thickness. Cut the dough into rounds using a floured plain 5 cm (2 inch) cutter. Place the scones close together on the prepared tray. Brush with a little milk. Bake for 10–12 minutes, or until golden brown. Serve warm with butter.

To make ½ cup of mashed pumpkin (winter squash) you will need around 250 g (9 oz) of raw pumpkin.

Chocolate Bread

Makes 2 loaves

2 teaspoons (7 g/^{1}/4 oz) dried yeast

55 g (2 oz/^{1}/4 cup) caster (superfine) sugar

90 g (3^1/4 oz/^{2}/3 cup) roughly chopped dark chocolate

50 g (1^3/4 oz) unsalted butter

375 g (13 oz/2^1/2 cups) strong flour

30 g (1 oz/^{1}/4 cup) unsweetened cocoa powder

1 egg, lightly beaten

^{1}/2 teaspoon natural vanilla extract

90 g (3^1/4 oz/^{1}/2 cup) dark chocolate chips

1 Sprinkle the yeast and a pinch of the sugar over 185 ml (6 fl oz/ ^{3}/4 cup) warm water in a small bowl. Stir to dissolve the sugar, then leave in a draught-free place for 10 minutes, or until bubbles appear on the surface.

2 Put the chocolate and butter in a heatproof bowl. Sit the bowl over a saucepan of simmering water, stirring frequently until the chocolate and butter have melted. Take care that the base of the bowl doesn't touch the water.

3 Combine the flour, cocoa powder, ^{1}/4 teaspoon salt and the remaining sugar in the bowl of an electric mixer with a dough-hook attachment.

4 Combine the egg and vanilla extract with the chocolate mixture, then pour the chocolate and yeast mixtures into the flour mixture. With the mixer set to the lowest speed, mix for 1–2 minutes, or until a dough forms. Increase the speed to medium and knead the dough for another 10 minutes, or until the dough is smooth and elastic. Alternatively, mix the dough by hand using a wooden spoon, then

turn out onto a floured work surface and knead for 10 minutes, or until the dough is smooth and elastic.

5. Transfer the dough to a large, oiled bowl, turning the dough to coat in the oil. Cover with plastic wrap and leave to rise in a warm place for 1½–2 hours, or until doubled in size.

6. Gently punch down the dough, then turn out onto a floured work surface. Divide the dough in half. Gently press out each half until 1 cm (½ inch) thick, then scatter the chocolate chips over each.

7. Roll up each piece of dough to form a log. Transfer to a greased baking tray. Cover with a damp tea (dish) towel and leave for 1 hour, or until doubled in size. Preheat the oven to 180°C (350°F/Gas 4).

8. Bake for 45–50 minutes, or until the loaves are light brown and sound hollow when tapped on the base. Transfer to a wire rack to cool.

This chocolate bread is not overly sweet. It is delicious served freshly sliced and spread with sweetened mascarpone cheese.

Hot Cross Buns

Makes 12

4 teaspoons (14 g/^{1}/$_2$ oz) dried yeast
500 g (1 lb 2 oz/3^1/$_3$ cups) strong flour
2 tablespoons caster (superfine) sugar
1 teaspoon mixed (pumpkin pie) spice
1 teaspoon ground cinnamon
40 g (1^1/$_4$ oz) butter
200 g (7 oz/1^2/$_3$ cups) sultanas (golden raisins)

CROSSES
30 g (1 oz/^{1}/$_4$ cup) plain (all-purpose) flour
^{1}/$_4$ teaspoon caster (superfine) sugar

GLAZE
1^1/$_2$ tablespoons caster (superfine) sugar
1 teaspoon powdered gelatine

1 Place the yeast, 2 teaspoons of the flour, 1 teaspoon of the sugar and
   125 ml (4 fl oz/^{1}/$_2$ cup) warm water in a small bowl and stir well.
   Leave in a warm, draught-free place for 10 minutes, or until bubbles
   appear on the surface. The mixture should be frothy and slightly
   increased in volume.

2 Sift the remaining flour and spices into a large bowl, stir in the sugar
   and rub in the butter with your fingertips. Stir in the sultanas. Make
   a well in the centre, stir in the yeast mixture and up to 185 ml
   (6 fl oz/^{3}/$_4$ cup) warm water to make a soft dough. Turn out onto
   a lightly floured surface and knead for 5 minutes, or until smooth,
   adding more flour if necessary, to prevent sticking.

3 Place the dough in a large floured bowl, cover with plastic wrap or a damp tea (dish) towel and leave in a warm place for about 30–40 minutes, or until doubled in size.

4 Preheat the oven to 200°C (400°F/Gas 6). Turn the dough out onto a lightly floured surface and knead gently to deflate. Divide into 12 portions and roll each into a ball. Place the balls on a lightly greased baking tray, just touching each other, in a rectangle three rolls wide and four rolls long. Cover loosely with plastic wrap or a damp tea towel and leave in a warm place for 20 minutes, or until nearly doubled in size.

5 To make the crosses, mix the flour, sugar and 2½ tablespoons water into a paste. Spoon into a paper piping bag and pipe crosses on top of the buns.

6 Bake for 20 minutes, or until golden brown. To make the glaze, put the sugar, gelatine and 1 tablespoon water in a small saucepan and stir over low heat until dissolved. Brush over the hot buns and leave to cool.

These spicy traditional Easter buns are heavily glazed and usually served warm or at room temperature. They are split open and buttered, or sometimes toasted.

Stollen

Makes 1

80 ml (2^1/$_2$ fl oz/^{1}/$_3$ cup) lukewarm milk

2 teaspoons sugar

2 teaspoons (7 g/^{1}/$_4$ oz) dried yeast

125 g (4^1/$_2$ oz) butter, softened

90 g (3^1/$_4$ oz/^{1}/$_3$ cup) caster (superfine) sugar

1 egg

2 teaspoons natural vanilla extract

^{1}/$_2$ teaspoon ground cinnamon

375 g (13 oz/2^1/$_2$ cups) strong flour

80 g (2^3/$_4$ oz/^{2}/$_3$ cup) raisins

75 g (2^1/$_2$ oz/^{1}/$_2$ cup) currants

95 g (3^1/$_4$ oz/^{1}/$_2$ cup) mixed peel

60 g (2^1/$_4$ oz/^{1}/$_2$ cup) slivered almonds

30 g (1 oz) butter, extra, melted

icing (confectioners') sugar, to dust

1   Put the milk, sugar, yeast and 80 ml (2^1/$_2$ fl oz/^{1}/$_3$ cup) warm water in a small bowl and mix well. Leave in a warm, draught-free place for 10 minutes, or until bubbles appear on the surface.

2   Beat the butter and sugar until light and creamy, then beat in the egg and vanilla extract. Add the yeast mixture, cinnamon and almost all the flour. Mix to a soft dough, adding more flour if necessary.

3   Turn out onto a lightly floured surface and knead for 10 minutes, or until the dough is smooth and elastic. Place in a lightly oiled bowl, cover with plastic wrap and leave in a warm place for 1 hour 45 minutes, or until doubled in size.

4   Punch down the dough and press it out to a thickness of about 1.5 cm (⁵⁄₈ inch). Sprinkle the fruit and almonds over the dough, then gather up and knead for a few minutes to mix the fruit and almonds evenly through the dough.

5   Shape the dough into an oval about 18 cm (7 inches) wide and 30 cm (12 inches) long. Fold in half lengthways, then press down to flatten slightly, with the fold slightly off centre on top of the loaf. Place on a greased baking tray, cover with plastic wrap and leave in a warm place for 1 hour, or until doubled in size.

6   Preheat the oven to 180°C (350°F/Gas 4). Bake for 40 minutes, or until golden. As soon as the bread is out of the oven, brush with the melted butter, allowing each brushing to be absorbed until you have used all the butter. Cool on a wire rack. Dust with icing sugar.

Stollen is a traditional German sweet yeast bread.

Rye Bread

Makes 1 loaf

2 teaspoons (7 g/^{1}/4 oz) dried yeast
1 teaspoon sugar
185 ml (6 fl oz/^{3}/4 cup) warm milk
200 g (7 oz/2 cups) rye flour
165 g (5^3/4 oz/1 heaped cup) strong flour
rye flour, extra, to dust

1 Place the yeast, sugar and milk in a small bowl and mix well. Leave in a warm place for 10 minutes, or until bubbles appear on the surface. The mixture should be frothy and slightly increased in volume.

2 Sift the flours and 1 teaspoon salt into a large bowl and make a well in the centre. Add the yeast mixture and 185 ml (6 fl oz/^{3}/4 cup) warm water and, using your fingers, gradually mix to form a dough.

3 Turn onto a lightly floured surface and knead for 10 minutes, or until smooth and elastic. Place the dough in a large lightly oiled bowl and cover with plastic wrap or a damp tea (dish) towel. Leave in a warm place for up to 1^1/2 hours, or until doubled in size.

4 Lightly grease a baking tray and dust lightly with flour. Punch down the dough and turn onto a lightly floured surface. Knead for a few minutes until smooth. Shape into an 18 cm (7 inch) circle and, using a sharp knife, score a cross on top of the loaf. Lightly dust the top with extra rye flour.

5 Cover the dough with plastic wrap and leave in a warm place for 1 hour, or until doubled in size. Preheat the oven to 180°C (350°F/Gas 4). Bake for 40–45 minutes, or until the bread is golden brown and sounds hollow when tapped. Transfer to a wire rack to cool.

Damper

Makes 1

375 g (13 oz/3 cups) self-raising flour
90 g (3¼ oz) butter, melted
125 ml (4 fl oz/½ cup) milk
milk, extra, to glaze
flour, extra, to dust

1 Preheat the oven to 210°C (415°F/Gas 6–7). Grease a baking tray. Sift the flour and 1–2 teaspoons salt into a bowl and make a well in the centre. Combine the butter, milk and 125 ml (4 fl oz/½ cup) water and pour into the well. Stir with a knife until just combined.

2 Turn the dough out onto a lightly floured surface and knead for 20 seconds, or until smooth. Place the dough on the baking tray and press out to a 20 cm (8 inch) circle. Using a sharp pointed knife, score the dough into eight sections about 1 cm (½ inch) deep. Brush with extra milk, then dust with extra flour.

3 Bake for 10 minutes. Reduce the oven temperature to 180°C (350°F/Gas 4) and bake for another 15 minutes, or until the damper is golden and sounds hollow when tapped.

Damper is the Australian version of soda bread. It is traditionally served warm with slatherings of golden syrup (honey, maple syrup or treacle can be substituted). If you prefer, you can make four rounds instead of one large damper and slightly reduce the cooking time.

Malt Bread

Makes 1 loaf

2 teaspoons (7 g/^{1}/4 oz) dried yeast

1 teaspoon sugar

300 g (10^1/2 oz/2 cups) wholemeal (whole-wheat) flour

125 g (4^1/2 oz/^{3}/4 cup) strong flour

2 teaspoons ground cinnamon

80 g (2^3/4 oz/^{2}/3 cup) raisins

30 g (1 oz) butter, melted

1 tablespoon treacle

1 tablespoon liquid malt extract

1 tablespoon hot milk

^{1}/2 teaspoon liquid malt extract, extra

1   Lightly grease a 21 x 14 x 7 cm (8^1/4 x 5^1/2 x 2^3/4 inch) loaf (bar) tin and line the base with baking paper.

2   Put the yeast, sugar and 250 ml (9 fl oz/1 cup) lukewarm water in a small bowl and stir until dissolved. Leave in a warm place for 10 minutes, or until bubbles appear on the surface. The mixture should be frothy and slightly increased in volume.

3   Sift the flours and cinnamon into a large bowl and add the raisins. Make a well in the centre and add the butter, treacle, malt and yeast mixture. Using a knife, mix to a soft dough.

4   Turn the dough out onto a lightly floured surface and knead for 10 minutes, or until smooth. Shape the dough into a ball and place in a lightly oiled bowl. Cover with plastic wrap or a damp tea (dish) towel and leave in a warm place for 1 hour, or until well risen.

5 Punch down the dough, then knead for 3 minutes, or until smooth. Roll the dough into a 20 cm (8 inch) square and roll up. Place, seam-side down, in the tin and set aside. Cover with plastic wrap or a damp tea towel and leave in a warm place for 40 minutes, or until risen.

6 Preheat the oven to 180°C (350°F/Gas 4). Brush the dough with the combined hot milk and extra malt. Bake for 40 minutes, or until well browned. Cool in the tin for 3 minutes before transferring to a wire rack to cool.

Malt bread is delicious sliced and spread with butter and honey.

Scones

Makes 10-12

310 g (11 oz/2½ cups) self-raising flour
1 teaspoon baking powder
40 g (1½ oz) unsalted butter, chilled and cubed
1 tablespoon sugar
250 ml (9 fl oz/1 cup) milk

1 Preheat the oven to 220°C (425°F/Gas 7). Lightly grease a baking tray or line it with baking paper.

2 Sift the flour, baking powder and a pinch of salt into a bowl. Rub in the butter briefly and lightly with your fingertips until the mixture is crumbly and resembles fine breadcrumbs. Mix in the sugar.

3 Make a well in the centre. Pour in almost all the milk and, with a flat-bladed knife and using a cutting action, mix until the dough comes together in clumps. Rotate the bowl as you work. Add the remaining milk if the mixture seems dry. Handle the mixture with great care and a very light hand. If you are heavy-handed and mix too much, or knead, your scones will be very tough. The dough should feel slightly wet and sticky.

4 With floured hands, gently gather the dough together, lift onto a lightly floured surface and pat into a smooth ball. Do not knead. Pat or lightly roll the dough out to 2 cm (¾ inch) thick. Using a floured 6 cm (2½ inch) cutter, cut into rounds. Gather the scraps together and, without handling too much, press out as before and cut out more rounds.

5   Place the rounds close together on the baking tray and lightly brush the tops with milk. Bake in the top half of the oven for 12–15 minutes, or until risen and golden. If you aren't sure they are cooked, break one open. If still doughy in the centre, cook for a few more minutes. For soft scones, wrap them in a dry tea (dish) towel while still hot. For scones with a crisp top, transfer to a wire rack to cool slightly before wrapping. Serve warm, or at room temperature, with butter or jam and whipped or clotted cream.

As scones contain little fat, they dry out quickly so are best eaten soon after baking. Otherwise they can be frozen. To make fruit scones, add 75 g (2¹/₂ oz/¹/₂ cup) currants or 85 g (3 oz/¹/₂ cup) chopped pitted dates to the mixture after you've rubbed in the butter. Mix well to distribute the fruit, then proceed with the recipe.

Sweet Yoghurt Plait

Makes 2 loaves

650 g (1 lb 7 oz/4^1/$_3$ cups) strong flour

1 tablespoon ground cinnamon

3 teaspoons (10 g/^{1}/$_4$ oz) dried yeast

2 eggs, lightly beaten

250 g (9 oz/1 cup) Greek-style yoghurt

125 ml (4 fl oz/^{1}/$_2$ cup) lukewarm milk

90 g (3^1/$_4$ oz/^{1}/$_4$ cup) honey

60 g (2^1/$_4$ oz) butter, melted

100 g (3^1/$_2$ oz/^{1}/$_2$ cup) chopped dried figs

GLAZE

1 egg

2 tablespoons milk

ICING

375 g (13 oz/3 cups) icing (confectioners') sugar, sifted

80 ml (2^1/$_2$ fl oz/^{1}/$_3$ cup) lemon juice

2 tablespoons boiling water

1   Combine 600 g (1 lb 5 oz/4 cups) of the flour, cinnamon, yeast and 1 teaspoon salt in the bowl of an electric mixer with a dough-hook attachment and make a well in the centre.

2   Combine the eggs, yoghurt, milk and honey in a bowl, then pour into the well. With the mixer set to the lowest speed, mix for 3 minutes to combine well. Increase the speed to medium and add the butter and figs and knead for 10 minutes, or until the dough is smooth and elastic; add the remaining flour if the mixture is still sticky. Alternatively, mix the dough by hand, using a wooden spoon, then

turn out onto a lightly floured work surface and knead for 10 minutes, or until smooth and elastic.

3 Transfer the dough to a large, oiled bowl, turning the dough to coat in the oil. Cover with plastic wrap and leave to rise in a warm place for 1 1/2 hours, or until doubled in size.

4 Gently punch down the dough, then turn out onto a floured work surface. Cut the dough into six equal portions, then roll each into 30 cm (12 inch) lengths. Plait three lengths of dough together, tucking the ends underneath for a neat finish. Repeat with the remaining dough lengths to make a second loaf.

5 Transfer to a large, lightly greased baking tray. Cover the tray with a damp tea (dish) towel and leave for 30 minutes, or until the dough has doubled in size. Preheat the oven to 220°C (425°F/Gas 7).

6 To make the glaze, mix together the egg and milk and brush over the tops of the loaves. Bake for 10 minutes, then reduce the oven temperature to 180°C (350°F/Gas 4) and bake for a further 20 minutes, or until the bread is golden and sounds hollow when tapped on the base. If the loaves start to brown too quickly, cover them with foil. Cool on a wire rack.

7 To make the icing, combine the icing sugar, lemon juice and boiling water in a bowl and, using a fork, stir until smooth. Drizzle over the cooled loaves. Set aside until the icing has set.

Pretzels

Makes 12

1 teaspoon dried yeast
1/4 teaspoon sugar
150 ml (5 fl oz) warm milk
185 g (6 1/2 oz/1 1/4 cups) strong flour
30 g (1 oz) butter, melted
1 egg yolk, lightly beaten
coarse sea salt, to sprinkle

1 Put the yeast, sugar and milk in a small bowl and stir well. Leave
   in a warm, draught-free place for 10 minutes, or until bubbles appear
   on the surface. The mixture should be frothy and slightly increased
   in volume.

2 Place the flour and 1/4 teaspoon salt in a large bowl and make a well in
   the centre. Add yeast mixture and butter and mix to a rough dough.
   Turn out onto a floured surface and knead for 10 minutes, until smooth
   and elastic. Transfer to an oiled bowl, roll in the oil, cover with plastic
   wrap and set aside in a warm place for 1 hour, or until doubled in size.

3 Preheat the oven to 190°C (375°F/Gas 5). Line a baking tray
   with baking paper. Punch down the dough and knead again for
   2–3 minutes. Divide into 12 pieces. Roll each piece into a long rope
   40 cm (16 inches) long. Circle and knot into a pretzel shape. Place
   well spaced on the baking tray and cover with a tea (dish) towel.
   Leave to rise in a warm place for 20–30 minutes.

4 Brush the pretzels with the egg yolk and sprinkle with sea salt. Place the
   pretzels in the oven and spray them twice with water before baking for
   12–15 minutes, or until crisp and golden. Transfer to a wire rack to cool.

Unleavened Lavash

Makes 4

125 g (4¹/2 oz/1 cup) plain (all-purpose) flour
¹/2 teaspoon sugar
20 g (³/4 oz) butter, chilled and cubed
80 ml (2¹/2 fl oz/¹/3 cup) milk
sesame and poppy seeds, to sprinkle

1. Put the flour, ¹/2 teaspoon salt, sugar and butter in a food processor. Process in short bursts until the butter is incorporated. With the motor running, gradually pour in the milk and process until the dough comes together—you may need to add an extra 1 tablespoon milk.

2. Turn out onto a lightly floured surface and knead briefly until smooth. Wrap in plastic wrap and refrigerate for 1 hour.

3. Preheat the oven to 190°C (375°F/Gas 5). Lightly grease a large baking tray. Cut the dough into four pieces. Working with one piece at a time, roll until very thin into a rough square shape measuring about 20 cm (8 inches) along the sides.

4. Place the dough squares on the baking tray, brush the tops lightly with water and sprinkle with the seeds. Roll a rolling pin lightly over the surface of the dough to press in the seeds. Bake for 6–8 minutes, or until golden brown and dry.

5. Transfer to a wire rack until cool and crisp. Break into large pieces. Repeat the process of rolling and baking the remaining dough.

Lavash is delicious served with dips or soft cheeses.

Saffron Buns

Makes 16

4 teaspoons (14 g/$^1/_2$ oz) dried yeast
500 ml (17 fl oz/2 cups) warm milk
$^1/_2$ teaspoon saffron threads
150 g (5$^1/_2$ oz) butter, cubed
875 g (1 lb 15 oz/5$^3/_4$ cups) strong flour
160 g (5$^1/_2$ oz/$^3/_4$ cup) sugar
160 g (5$^1/_2$ oz/1$^1/_3$ cups) raisins
2 eggs, lightly beaten

1   Combine the yeast, 125 ml (4 fl oz/$^1/_2$ cup) of the milk and the saffron in a small bowl and stir well. Leave in a warm draught-free place for 10 minutes, or until bubbles appear on the surface. The mixture should be frothy and slightly increased in volume.

2   Melt the butter in a small saucepan, add the remaining milk and stir over low heat until warm. Remove from the heat and cover.

3   Sift the flour and 1 teaspoon salt into a large bowl, stir in the sugar and half the raisins, then make a well in the centre. Add the just-warm saffron milk mixture and half the beaten egg. Mix with a flat-bladed knife, using a cutting action, until the mixture comes together to form a soft dough.

4   Turn out onto a lightly floured work surface and knead for 5–7 minutes, or until smooth. Place the dough in a large, lightly oiled bowl, cover with plastic wrap or a damp tea (dish) towel, and leave for 1–1$^1/_2$ hours in a warm place, or until doubled in size.

5 Turn the dough out onto a lightly floured work surface and knead for 5 minutes. Cut into 16 portions. Roll each portion into a sausage shape about 20 cm (8 inches) long and form each into an 'S' shape. Place on greased baking trays. Cover loosely with plastic wrap or a damp tea towel and leave in a warm place for 30 minutes, or until doubled in size. Preheat the oven to 200°C (400°F/Gas 6).

6 Brush the buns with the remaining beaten egg and decorate with the remaining raisins, placing them gently into the 'S' shapes, being careful not to deflate the buns. Bake for 10 minutes, or until the tops are brown and the buns feel hollow when tapped underneath. Transfer to a wire rack to cool. Serve warm or cold, plain or buttered.

apple and spice teacake butterfly cupcakes

Cakes and muffins

olate mud cake classic sponge pound cake

Angel Food Cake with Chocolate Sauce

Makes 1

125 g (4$^{1/2}$ oz/1 cup) plain (all-purpose) flour

250 g (9 oz/1 heaped cup) caster (superfine) sugar

10 egg whites, at room temperature

1 teaspoon cream of tartar

$^{1/2}$ teaspoon natural vanilla extract

CHOCOLATE SAUCE

250 g (9 oz/1$^{2/3}$ cups) chopped dark chocolate

185 ml (6 fl oz/$^{3/4}$ cup) pouring (whipping) cream

50 g (1$^{3/4}$ oz) unsalted butter, cubed

1   Preheat the oven to 180°C (350°F/Gas 4). Have an ungreased angel cake tin ready.

2   Sift the flour and 125 g (4$^{1/2}$ oz/$^{1/2}$ cup) of the sugar four times into a large bowl. Set aside.

3   Beat the egg whites, cream of tartar and $^{1/4}$ teaspoon salt in a clean, large bowl with electric beaters until soft peaks form. Gradually add the remaining sugar and beat until thick and glossy. Add the vanilla extract.

4   Sift half the flour and sugar mixture over the meringue and gently fold into the mixture with a metal spoon. Repeat with the remaining flour and sugar.

5   Spoon into the cake tin and bake for 45 minutes, or until a skewer comes out clean when inserted into the centre of the cake. Gently loosen around the side of the cake with a spatula, then turn the cake out onto a wire rack to cool completely.

6 To make the chocolate sauce, put the chocolate, cream and butter in a saucepan. Stir over low heat until the chocolate has melted and the mixture is smooth. Drizzle over the cake and serve.

 Ensure the tin is very clean and not greased or the cake will not rise but slip down the side of the tin.

Date and Walnut Rolls

Makes 2

90 g (3¹/4 oz/³/4 cup) self-raising flour

90 g (3¹/4 oz/³/4 cup) plain (all-purpose) flour

¹/2 teaspoon bicarbonate of soda (baking soda)

1 teaspoon mixed (pumpkin pie) spice

125 g (4¹/2 oz/1 cup) chopped walnuts

100 g (3¹/2 oz) unsalted butter, cubed

140 g (5 oz/³/4 cup) soft brown sugar

280 g (10 oz/1³/4 cups) chopped pitted dates

1 egg, lightly beaten

1 Preheat the oven to 180°C (350°F/Gas 4). Lightly grease two 17 x 8 cm (6¹/2 x 3¹/4 inch) Swiss (jelly) roll tins and their lids.

2 Sift the flours, bicarbonate of soda and mixed spice into a large bowl, then stir in the walnuts. Make a well in the centre.

3 Combine the butter, sugar, dates and 125 ml (4 oz/¹/2 cup) water in a saucepan. Stir constantly over low heat until the butter has melted and the sugar has dissolved. Remove from the heat and set aside to cool slightly. Add the butter mixture and egg to the flour and stir well.

4 Spoon the mixture evenly into the prepared tins. Bake, with the tins upright on a baking tray, for 1 hour, or until a skewer comes out clean when inserted into the centre of the loaves. Leave in the tins, with the lids on, for 10 minutes before turning out onto a wire rack to cool. Serve in slices, buttered.

Apple and Spice Teacake

Makes 1

180 g (6 oz) unsalted butter, softened
95 g (3^{1}/4 oz/^{1}/2 cup) soft brown sugar
2 teaspoons finely grated lemon zest
3 eggs, lightly beaten
125 g (4^{1}/2 oz/1 cup) self-raising flour
75 g (2^{1}/2 oz/^{1}/2 cup) wholemeal (whole-wheat) flour
^{1}/2 teaspoon ground cinnamon
125 ml (4 fl oz/^{1}/2 cup) milk
410 g (14^{1}/2 oz/2 cups) tinned pie apple
^{1}/4 teaspoon mixed (pumpkin pie) spice
1 tablespoon soft brown sugar, extra
25 g (1 oz/^{1}/4 cup) flaked almonds

1   Preheat the oven to 180°C (350°F/Gas 4). Grease a 20 cm (8 inch) spring-form cake tin and line the base with baking paper. Cream the butter and sugar in a bowl with electric beaters until light and fluffy. Beat in the lemon zest. Add the eggs gradually, beating thoroughly after each addition. Transfer the mixture to a large bowl. Fold in the sifted flours and cinnamon alternately with the milk. Stir until smooth.

2   Spoon half the mixture into the prepared tin, top with three-quarters of the apple, then the remaining cake mixture. Press the remaining apple around the edge of the top. Combine the mixed spice, extra sugar and flaked almonds and sprinkle over the cake.

3   Bake for 1 hour, or until a skewer comes out clean when inserted into the centre of the cake. Leave in the tin for 15 minutes before turning out onto a wire rack to cool.

Banana Cake

Makes 1

125 g (4¹/2 oz) unsalted butter, softened

125 g (4¹/2 oz/¹/2 cup) caster (superfine) sugar

2 eggs, lightly beaten

1 teaspoon natural vanilla extract

4 ripe bananas, mashed

1 teaspoon bicarbonate of soda (baking soda)

125 ml (4 fl oz/¹/2 cup) milk

250 g (9 oz/2 cups) self-raising flour, sifted

¹/2 teaspoon mixed (pumpkin pie) spice

BUTTER FROSTING

125 g (4¹/2 oz) unsalted butter, softened

90 g (3¹/4 oz/³/4 cup) icing (confectioners') sugar

1 tablespoon lemon juice

15 g (¹/2 oz/¹/4 cup) flaked coconut, toasted

1   Preheat the oven to 180°C (350°F/Gas 4). Lightly grease a 20 cm (8 inch) round cake tin and line the base with baking paper.

2   Cream the butter and sugar in a small bowl with electric beaters until light and fluffy. Add the eggs gradually, beating thoroughly after each addition. Add the vanilla extract and banana and beat until combined. Transfer to a large bowl.

3   Dissolve the bicarbonate of soda in the milk. Using a metal spoon, gently fold the sifted flour and mixed spice alternately with the milk into the banana mixture. Stir until all the ingredients are just combined and the mixture is smooth. Spoon into the prepared tin

and smooth the surface. Bake for 1 hour, or until a skewer comes out clean when inserted into the centre of the cake. Leave in the tin for 10 minutes before turning out onto a wire rack to cool completely.

4 To make the butter frosting, beat the butter, icing sugar and lemon juice with electric beaters until smooth and creamy. Spread over the cooled cake using a flat-bladed knife and sprinkle with toasted coconut flakes.

 Very ripe bananas are best for this recipe as they have the most developed flavour.

Butter Cake

Makes 1

185 g (6½ oz/1½ cups) self-raising flour
60 g (2¼ oz/½ cup) plain (all-purpose) flour
185 g (6½ oz) unsalted butter, softened
185 g (6½ oz/heaped ¾ cup) caster (superfine) sugar
3 eggs, lightly beaten
1 teaspoon natural vanilla extract
60 ml (2 fl oz/¼ cup) milk

1 Preheat the oven to 180°C (375°F/Gas 4). Sift the flours into a bowl. Cream the butter and sugar in a small bowl with electric beaters until light and fluffy, scraping the side of the bowl with a spatula several times. The mixture will almost double in volume and should have no trace of the sugar granules. This initial creaming process can take up to 8 minutes.

2 With the beaters still running, gradually add the egg, a little at a time, beating thoroughly after each addition. Add the vanilla extract and beat well to combine. Transfer the mixture to a large bowl. Using a large metal spoon, gently fold in the sifted flour and the milk. Stir until just combined and almost smooth, mixing lightly and evenly.

3 Gently spoon or pour the mixture into a greased 20 cm (8 inch) cake tin, spread out evenly and smooth the surface. Bake for 45 minutes. The cake is cooked when it begins to shrink from the side of the tin and is lightly golden. If gently pressed with a finger, it should spring back into shape. As a final check, insert a fine skewer in the centre— it should come out clean, without any moisture. Avoid opening the oven door until at least two-thirds of the way through baking.

Butterfly Cupcakes

Makes 12

120 g (4$^{1}/_{4}$ oz) unsalted butter, softened
180 g (6$^{1}/_{2}$ oz/$^{3}/_{4}$ cup) caster (superfine) sugar
185 g (6$^{1}/_{2}$ oz/1$^{1}/_{2}$ cups) self-raising flour
125 ml (4 fl oz/$^{1}/_{2}$ cup) milk
2 eggs
125 ml (4 fl oz/$^{1}/_{2}$ cup) thick (double/heavy) cream
strawberry jam, to decorate
icing (confectioners') sugar, to dust

1   Preheat the oven to 180°C (350°F/Gas 4). Line a flat-bottomed
    12-hole cupcake tray with paper cases.

2   Beat the butter, sugar, flour, milk and eggs with electric beaters on
    low speed. Increase the speed and beat until smooth and pale. Divide
    evenly among the paper cases and bake for 30 minutes, or until
    cooked and golden. Transfer to a wire rack to cool.

3   Cut shallow rounds from the centre of each cake using the point of
    a sharp knife, then cut in half. Spoon 2 teaspoons cream into each
    cavity, top with a small dollop of strawberry jam, then position two
    halves of the cake tops in the jam to resemble butterfly wings. Dust
    with icing sugar.

Chocolate Mud Cake

Makes 1

125 g (4¹/2 oz/1 cup) plain (all-purpose) flour
125 g (4¹/2 oz/1 cup) self-raising flour
60 g (2¹/2 oz/¹/2 cup) unsweetened cocoa powder
¹/2 teaspoon bicarbonate of soda (baking soda)
625 g (1 lb 6 oz/2³/4 cups) sugar
450 g (1 lb/3 cups) chopped dark chocolate
450 g (1 lb) unsalted butter
125 ml (4 fl oz/¹/2 cup) buttermilk
2 tablespoons oil
2 tablespoons instant coffee granules or powder
4 eggs

1 Preheat the oven to 160°C (315°F/Gas 2–3). Brush a deep 23 cm (9 inch) square cake tin with melted butter. Line the base and sides with baking paper, extending at least 2 cm (³/4 inches) above the rim.

2 Sift the flours, cocoa and bicarbonate of soda into a large bowl. Stir in the sugar and make a well in the centre. Put 250 g (9 oz/1²/3 cups) of the chocolate and 250 g (9 oz/1 cup) of the butter in a saucepan. Add 185 ml (6 fl oz/³/4 cup) water and stir over low heat until melted. Stir the chocolate mixture into the dry ingredients using a large metal spoon.

3 Whisk together the buttermilk, oil, coffee and eggs in a large jug and add to the mixture, stirring until smooth. Pour into the tin and bake for 1 hour 40 minutes, or until a skewer comes out clean when inserted into the centre of the cake. Cool in the tin, then turn out.

4   Combine the remaining chocolate and butter in a small saucepan and
    stir over low heat until smooth. Cool to room temperature, stirring
    often, until thick enough to spread. Turn the cake upside down so
    that the uneven top becomes the base, and spread the icing over the
    entire cake. Allow the icing to set slightly before serving.

 For best results when baking a cake,
position an oven rack in the lower third
of the oven so the top of the cake is in the
middle of the oven. Centre the cake tin on
the oven rack.

Black Forest Cake

Makes 1

200 g (7 oz) unsalted butter, softened

185 g (6^1/$_2$ oz/heaped ^{3}/$_4$ cup) caster (superfine) sugar

3 eggs, lightly beaten

1 teaspoon natural vanilla extract

210 g (7^1/$_2$ oz/1^2/$_3$ cups) self-raising flour

40 g (1^1/$_2$ oz/^{1}/$_3$ cup) plain (all-purpose) flour

90 g (3^1/$_4$ oz/^{3}/$_4$ cup) unsweetened cocoa powder

1 tablespoon instant coffee powder

^{1}/$_2$ teaspoon bicarbonate of soda (baking soda)

125 ml (4 fl oz/^{1}/$_2$ cup) buttermilk

80 ml (2^1/$_2$ fl oz/^{1}/$_3$ cup) milk

315 ml (10^3/$_4$ fl oz/1^1/$_4$ cups) pouring (whipping) cream

425 g (15 oz) tinned pitted cherries, drained

chocolate curls, for decoration

CHOCOLATE TOPPING

300 g (10^1/$_2$ oz) dark chocolate, chopped

375 g (13 oz) unsalted butter, softened

1 Preheat the oven to 180°C (350°F/Gas 4). Grease a 23 cm (9 inch) round cake tin and line the base and side with baking paper.

2 Cream the butter and sugar in a small bowl with electric beaters until light and fluffy. Add the egg gradually, beating thoroughly after each addition. Add the vanilla extract and beat until well combined.

3 Transfer the mixture to a large bowl. Using a metal spoon, fold in the sifted flours, cocoa, coffee and bicarbonate of soda with the combined buttermilk and milk. Stir until just combined and almost smooth.

4   Pour the mixture into the tin and smooth the surface. Bake for 40–50 minutes, or until a skewer comes out clean when inserted into the centre of the cake. Leave in the tin for 20 minutes before turning out onto a wire rack to cool.

5   To make the chocolate topping, bring a saucepan of water to the boil and remove from the heat. Place the chocolate in a heatproof bowl and sit the bowl over the pan, making sure the bowl is not touching the water. Allow to stand, stirring occasionally, until the chocolate has melted. Beat the butter in a small bowl until light and creamy. Add the chocolate, beating for 1 minute, or until the mixture is glossy and smooth.

6   Whip the cream. Turn the cake upside down and cut into three layers horizontally. Place the first layer on a serving plate and spread evenly with half the whipped cream, then top with half the cherries. Continue layering with the remaining cake, cream and cherries, ending with the cake on the top. Spread the chocolate topping over the top and side, using a flat-bladed knife. Using a piping bag, pipe swirls with the remaining topping around the cake rim. Decorate with chocolate curls.

 This cake is best assembled and eaten on the day that it is made.

Madeleines

Makes 14 (or 30 small ones)

3 eggs
100 g (3¹/₂ oz/¹/₂ cup) caster (superfine) sugar
150 g (5¹/₂ oz/1¹/₄ cups) plain (all-purpose) flour
100 g (3¹/₂ oz) unsalted butter, melted
grated zest of 1 lemon
grated zest of 1 orange

1 Preheat the oven to 200°C (400°F/Gas 6). Brush a tray of madeleine moulds with melted butter and coat with flour, then tap the tray to remove the excess flour.

2 Whisk the eggs and sugar until the mixture is thick and pale and the whisk leaves a trail when lifted. Gently fold in the flour, then the butter and lemon and orange zest.

3 Spoon the mixture into the moulds, leaving a little room for rising. Bake for 12 minutes (small madeleines will only need 7 minutes), or until very lightly golden and springy to the touch. Remove from the tray and cool on a wire rack.

Chocolate Ginger and Fig Cake

Makes 1

125 g (4¹/2 oz) unsalted butter, softened

230 g (8 oz/1 cup firmly packed) soft brown sugar

2 eggs, lightly beaten

185 g (6¹/2 oz/1¹/2 cups) self-raising flour

40 g (1¹/2 oz/¹/3 cup) unsweetened cocoa powder

185 ml (6 fl oz/³/4 cup) milk

125 g (4¹/2 oz/²/3 cup) dried figs, chopped

75 g (2¹/2 oz/¹/3 cup) glacé (candied) ginger, chopped

1 Preheat the oven to 180°C (350°F/Gas 4). Grease a 22 x 12 cm (8¹/2 x 4¹/2 inch) loaf (bar) tin and line the base with baking paper.

2 Cream the butter and sugar with electric beaters until light and fluffy. Gradually add the egg, beating well after each addition. Stir in the sifted flour and cocoa alternately with the milk to make a smooth batter. Fold in the figs and half the ginger.

3 Spoon the mixture into the prepared tin and smooth the surface. Scatter the remaining ginger over the top. Bake for 1 hour, or until a skewer comes out clean when inserted into the centre of the cake. Leave the cake to cool in the tin for 5 minutes before turning out onto a wire rack.

Pistachio Friands

Makes 10

165 g (5³/4 oz/1¹/3 cups) icing (confectioners') sugar
40 g (1¹/2 oz/¹/3 cup) plain (all-purpose) flour
125 g (4¹/2 oz/1 cup) ground pistachios
160 g (5³/4 oz) unsalted butter, melted
5 egg whites, lightly beaten
¹/2 teaspoon natural vanilla extract
55 g (2 oz/¹/4 cup) caster (superfine) sugar
35 g (1¹/4 oz/¹/4 cup) chopped pistachios
icing (confectioners') sugar, to dust

1 Preheat the oven to 190°C (375°F/Gas 5). Lightly grease ten 125 ml (4 fl oz/¹/2 cup) friand tins.

2 Sift the icing sugar and flour into a bowl. Add the ground pistachios, butter, egg whites and vanilla extract and stir with a metal spoon until just combined.

3 Spoon the mixture into the prepared tins, place on a baking tray and bake for 15–20 minutes, or until a skewer inserted into the centre of a friand comes out clean. Leave in the tins for 5 minutes, then turn out onto a wire rack to cool.

4 Meanwhile, put the caster sugar and 60 ml (2 fl oz/¹/4 cup) water in a small saucepan and stir over low heat until the sugar has dissolved. Increase the heat, then boil for 4 minutes, or until thick and syrupy. Remove from the heat and stir in the chopped pistachios, then, working quickly, spoon the mixture over the tops of the friands. Dust with icing sugar to serve.

Classic Sponge

Makes 1 layered sponge

75 g (2¹/2 oz/heaped ¹/2 cup) plain (all-purpose) flour
150 g (5¹/2 oz/1¹/4 cups) self-raising flour
6 eggs
220 g (7³/4 oz/1 cup) caster (superfine) sugar
2 tablespoons boiling water
160 g (5³/4 oz/¹/2 cup) strawberry jam
250 ml (9 fl oz/1 cup) pouring (whipping) cream
icing (confectioners') sugar, to dust

1   Preheat the oven to 180°C (350°F/Gas 4). Lightly grease two
    22 cm (8¹/2 inch) round cake tins and line the bases with baking
    paper. Dust the tins with a little flour, shaking off any excess.

2   Sift the flours together three times onto a sheet of baking paper.
    Beat the eggs in a large bowl with electric beaters for 7 minutes, or
    until thick and pale. Gradually add the sugar to the eggs, beating well
    after each addition. Using a large metal spoon, quickly and gently
    fold in the sifted flour and boiling water.

3   Spread the mixture evenly into the tins and bake for 25 minutes, or
    until the sponges are lightly golden and shrink slightly from the sides
    of the tins. Leave in the tins for 5 minutes before turning out onto a
    wire rack to cool.

4   Spread the jam over one of the sponges. Whip the cream in a small
    bowl until stiff peaks form, then spoon into a piping bag and pipe
    rosettes over the jam. Place the other sponge on top. Dust with
    icing sugar.

Carrot Cake

Makes 1

125 g (4^1/$_2$ oz/1 cup) self-raising flour

125 g (4^1/$_2$ oz/1 cup) plain (all-purpose) flour

2 teaspoons ground cinnamon

1 teaspoon ground ginger

^{1}/$_2$ teaspoon ground nutmeg

1 teaspoon bicarbonate of soda (baking soda)

250 ml (9 fl oz/1 cup) oil

185 g (6^1/$_2$ oz/1 cup) soft brown sugar

4 eggs

175 g (6 oz/^{1}/$_2$ cup) golden syrup (or substitute honey, maple syrup
or treacle)

400 g (14 oz/2^2/$_3$ cups) grated carrot

60 g (2^1/$_4$ oz/^{1}/$_2$ cup) chopped pecans or walnuts

LEMON ICING

175 g (6 oz/^{3}/$_4$ cup) cream cheese, softened

60 g (2^1/$_4$ oz) butter, softened

185 g (6^1/$_2$ oz/1^1/$_2$ cups) icing (confectioners') sugar

1 teaspoon natural vanilla extract

1–2 teaspoons lemon juice

1   Preheat the oven to 160°C (315°F/Gas 2–3). Lightly grease a 23 cm
(9 inch) round cake tin and line the base and side with baking paper.

2   Sift the flours, spices and bicarbonate of soda into a large bowl and
make a well in the centre.

3 Whisk together the oil, sugar, eggs and golden syrup in a jug until combined. Add this mixture to the dry ingredients and gradually stir with a metal spoon until smooth. Stir in the carrot and nuts, then spoon into the prepared tin and smooth the surface.

4 Bake for 1 hour 30 minutes, or until a skewer comes out clean when inserted into the centre of the cake. Leave in the tin for at least 15 minutes before turning out onto a wire rack to cool completely.

5 To make the lemon icing, beat the cream cheese and butter with electric beaters until smooth. Gradually add the icing sugar alternately with the vanilla extract and lemon juice, beating until light and creamy. Spread the icing over the cooled cake using a flat-bladed knife.

 If you prefer, cut the cake in half horizontally, then sandwich the layers together with half the icing. The top can be sprinkled with freshly grated nutmeg.

Chocolate Cake

Makes 1

125 g (4¹/2 oz) unsalted butter, softened
125 g (4¹/2 oz/heaped ¹/2 cup) caster (superfine) sugar
40 g (1¹/2 oz/¹/3 cup) icing (confectioners') sugar, sifted
2 eggs, lightly beaten
1 teaspoon natural vanilla extract
80 g (2³/4 oz/¹/4 cup) blackberry jam
155 g (5¹/2 oz/1¹/4 cups) self-raising flour
60 g (2¹/4 oz/¹/2 cup) unsweetened cocoa powder
1 teaspoon bicarbonate of soda (baking soda)
250 ml (9 fl oz/1 cup) milk

CHOCOLATE BUTTERCREAM
50 g (1³/4 oz/¹/3 cup) finely chopped dark chocolate
25 g (1 oz) unsalted butter
3 teaspoons pouring (whipping) cream
30 g (1 oz/¹/4 cup) icing (confectioners') sugar, sifted

1   Preheat the oven to 180°C (350°F/Gas 4). Lightly grease a 20 cm
    (8 inch) square cake tin and line with baking paper.

2   Cream the butter and sugars in a small bowl with electric beaters until
    light and fluffy. Add the eggs gradually, beating thoroughly after each
    addition. Beat in the vanilla extract and jam. Transfer to a large bowl.
    Using a metal spoon, gently fold in the combined sifted flour, cocoa and
    bicarbonate of soda with the milk. Stir until the mixture is smooth.

3   Pour the mixture into the prepared tin and smooth the surface. Bake
    for 45 minutes, or until a skewer comes out clean. Leave in the tin for
    15 minutes before turning out onto a wire rack to cool completely.

4 To make the chocolate butter cream, stir all the ingredients in a small saucepan over low heat until smooth and glossy. Spread over the top of the cake with a flat-bladed knife.

The cake is cooked when it begins to shrink from the side of the tin—if gently pressed with a finger, it should spring back into shape.

Apricot Pine Nut Cake

Makes 1

100 g (3 1/2 oz/2/3 cup) pine nuts, roughly chopped

250 g (9 oz) unsalted butter, softened

250 g (9 oz/1 heaped cup) sugar

3 teaspoons finely grated orange zest

3 eggs, lightly beaten

310 g (11 oz/2 1/2 cups) self-raising flour, sifted

200 g (7 oz/3/4 cup) finely chopped glacé (candied) apricots

250 ml (9 fl oz/1 cup) orange juice

1   Preheat the oven to 180°C (350°F/Gas 4). Lightly grease a 26 cm (10 1/2 inch) round cake tin and line the base with baking paper. Spread the pine nuts on a baking tray and bake for 5–10 minutes, or until lightly golden. Leave to cool.

2   Cream the butter, sugar and orange zest with electric beaters until light and fluffy. Add the egg gradually, beating well after each addition—the mixture may look curdled but once you add the flour, it will bring it back together. Fold in the sifted flour, pine nuts, apricots and orange juice in two batches with a metal spoon. Spoon the mixture into the prepared tin and smooth the surface.

3   Bake for 1 hour 20 minutes, or until a skewer comes out clean when inserted into the centre of the cake. Leave in the tin for 10 minutes before turning out onto a wire rack to cool. If desired, dust with icing sugar and serve with cream or yoghurt.

Apple Cinnamon Muffins

Makes 12

400 g (14 oz/2 cups) tinned pie apple

310 g (11 oz/2^{1}/2 cups) self-raising flour

2 teaspoons ground cinnamon

125 g (4^{1}/2 oz/^{2}/3 cup) soft brown sugar

350 ml (12 fl oz) milk

2 eggs

1 teaspoon natural vanilla extract

150 g (5^{1}/2 oz) unsalted butter, melted and cooled

60 g (2^{1}/4 oz/^{1}/2 cup) walnuts, finely chopped

1. Preheat the oven to 200°C (400°F/Gas 6). Lightly grease twelve 125 ml (4 fl oz/^{1}/2 cup) muffin holes. Place the pie apple in a bowl and break up with a knife.

2. Sift the flour and cinnamon into a bowl and add the sugar. Make a well in the centre. Whisk together the milk, eggs and vanilla extract in a jug and pour into the well. Add the melted butter.

3. Fold the mixture gently with a metal spoon until just combined. Add the apple filling and gently stir through. Do not over-mix—the batter should be lumpy.

4. Fill each muffin hole with the mixture (the holes will be quite full, but these muffins don't rise as much as some) and sprinkle with walnuts.

5. Bake for 20–25 minutes, or until the muffins are risen, golden and come away slightly from the tin. Allow to cool for a couple of minutes, then gently loosen each muffin with a flat-bladed knife and transfer to a wire rack. Serve warm or at room temperature.

Orange and Lemon Syrup Cake

Makes 1

3 lemons

3 oranges

250 g (9 oz) unsalted butter, chilled and cubed

685 g (1 lb 8 oz/3 cups) caster (superfine) sugar

6 eggs, lightly beaten

375 ml (13 fl oz/1½ cups) milk

375 g (13 oz/3 cups) self-raising flour, sifted

1 Preheat the oven to 160°C (315°F/Gas 2–3). Grease a 24 cm (9½ inch) spring-form cake tin and line the base and side with baking paper.

2 Finely grate the zest of the lemons and oranges to give 3 tablespoons of each, then squeeze the fruit to give 185 ml (6 fl oz/¾ cup) juice from each. Heat the butter, 500 g (1 lb 2 oz/2 cups) of the sugar and 1 tablespoon each of the lemon and orange zest in a saucepan over low heat, stirring until melted. Pour into a bowl.

3 Add half the egg, 185 ml (6 fl oz/¾ cup) of the milk and 185 g (6½ oz/1½ cups) of the flour, beating with electric beaters until just combined. Add the remaining egg, milk and flour and beat until smooth—do not overmix. Pour into the prepared tin and bake for 1 hour 15 minutes, or until a skewer comes out clean when inserted into the centre of the cake—cover with foil if it browns too much. Cool in the tin.

4 Combine the fruit juices, the remaining zest and sugar and 125 ml (4 fl oz/½ cup) water in a saucepan and stir over low heat until the sugar has dissolved. Increase the heat and boil for 10 minutes, or until it thickens and reduces slightly. Pour the hot syrup over the cool cake. Cool in the tin for 10 minutes, then remove.

Pound Cake

Makes 1

375 g (13 oz) unsalted butter, softened

375 g (13 oz/1²/₃ cups) caster (superfine) sugar

1 teaspoon natural vanilla extract

6 eggs, lightly beaten

375 g (13 oz/3 cups) plain (all-purpose) flour, sifted

1 teaspoon baking powder

60 ml (2 fl oz/¼ cup) milk

icing (confectioners') sugar, to dust

1   Preheat the oven to 180°C (350°F/Gas 4). Lightly grease the base and side of a 22 cm (8½ inch) round cake tin and line the base with baking paper.

2   Cream the butter and sugar in a small bowl with electric beaters until light and fluffy. Beat in the vanilla extract, then add the eggs gradually, beating thoroughly after each addition. Transfer to a large bowl. Using a metal spoon, fold in the sifted flour and baking powder alternately with the milk. Do this in three or four batches. Stir until the mixture is just combined and almost smooth.

3   Spoon the mixture into the prepared tin and smooth the surface. Bake for 1 hour, or until a skewer comes out clean when inserted into the centre of the cake. Leave in the tin for 10 minutes before turning out onto a wire rack to cool. Lightly dust the top with icing sugar just before serving.

Fig and Raspberry Cake

Makes 1

185 g (6^1/$_2$ oz) unsalted butter

185 g (6^1/$_2$ oz/heaped ^{3}/$_4$ cup) caster (superfine) sugar

1 egg

1 egg yolk, extra

335 g (11^3/$_4$ oz/2^2/$_3$ cups) plain (all-purpose) flour

1 teaspoon baking powder

4 fresh figs, quartered

grated zest of 1 orange

200 g (7 oz/1^2/$_3$ cups) raspberries

2 tablespoons sugar

1　Preheat the oven to 180°C (350°F/Gas 4). Cream the butter and sugar in a bowl until light and fluffy. Add the whole egg and egg yolk and beat again.

2　Sift the flour over the bowl and fold in with the baking powder and a pinch of salt. Chill for 15 minutes, or until firm enough to roll out.

3　Lightly grease a 23 cm (9 inch) spring-form cake tin. Divide the dough in two and roll out one piece large enough to fit the base of the tin. Cover with the figs, orange zest and raspberries. Roll out the remaining dough and fit it over the filling. Lightly brush the dough with water and sprinkle with the sugar.

4　Bake for 30 minutes, or until a skewer comes out clean when inserted into the centre of the cake. Serve with cream or mascarpone cheese.

Gingerbread Apricot Upside-down Cake

Makes 1

200 g (7 oz) glacé (candied) apricots

175 g (6 oz) unsalted butter

30 g (1 oz/¼ cup) pecans, finely chopped

165 g (5¾ oz/¾ cup firmly packed) soft brown sugar

90 g (3¼ oz/¼ cup) golden syrup (or substitute honey, maple syrup or treacle)

185 g (6½ oz/1½ cups) self-raising flour

3 teaspoons ground ginger

½ teaspoon ground nutmeg

1   Preheat the oven to 180°C (350°F/Gas 4). Grease and flour the base of a deep 20 cm (8 inch) round cake tin, shaking out the excess flour.

2   Arrange the apricots around the base of the tin, cut side up. Melt the butter in a small saucepan over low heat. Transfer 1 tablespoon of the melted butter to a small bowl. Add the pecans and 55 g (2 oz/¼ cup) of the sugar and mix well. Sprinkle the mixture over the apricots.

3   Add the golden syrup and 125 ml (4 fl oz/½ cup) water to the saucepan of melted butter and stir over medium heat until well combined. Sift the flour and spices into a bowl, then stir in the remaining sugar. Pour in the golden syrup mixture and mix well. Spoon the mixture over the apricots and smooth the surface.

4   Bake for 35–40 minutes, or until a skewer comes out clean when inserted into the centre of the cake. Leave in the tin for 15 minutes before turning out onto a wire rack to cool. If desired, serve with custard.

Saffron Spice Cake

Makes 1

250 ml (9 fl oz/1 cup) fresh orange juice
1 tablespoon finely grated orange zest
1/4 teaspoon saffron threads
3 eggs
155 g (5 1/2 oz/1 1/4 cups) icing (confectioners') sugar
250 g (9 oz/2 cups) self-raising flour
370 g (13 oz/3 2/3 cups) ground almonds
125 g (4 1/2 oz) unsalted butter, melted
icing (confectioners') sugar, extra, to dust
thick (double/heavy) cream, to serve

1 Preheat the oven to 180°C (350°F/Gas 4). Lightly grease a 22 cm (8 1/2 inch) round cake tin and line the base with baking paper.

2 Combine the orange juice, orange zest and saffron in a small saucepan and bring to the boil. Lower the heat and simmer for 1 minute. Leave to cool.

3 Beat the eggs and icing sugar with electric beaters until light and creamy. Fold in the sifted flour, almonds, orange juice mixture and butter with a metal spoon until just combined and the mixture is just smooth. Spoon the mixture into the prepared tin.

4 Bake for 1 hour, or until a skewer comes out clean when inserted into the centre of the cake. Leave in the tin for 15 minutes before turning out onto a wire rack to cool. Dust with a little icing sugar and serve with cream.

Lemon Coconut Cake

Makes 1

185 g (6$^{1}/_{2}$ oz/1$^{1}/_{2}$ cups) self-raising flour
45 g (1$^{1}/_{2}$ oz/$^{1}/_{2}$ cup) desiccated coconut
1 tablespoon grated lemon zest
250 g (9 oz/1 heaped cup) caster (superfine) sugar
125 g (4$^{1}/_{2}$ oz) unsalted butter, melted
2 eggs
250 ml (9 fl oz/1 cup) milk

COCONUT ICING
185 g (6$^{1}/_{2}$ oz/1$^{1}/_{2}$ cups) icing (confectioners') sugar, sifted
90 g (3$^{1}/_{4}$ oz/1 cup) desiccated coconut
$^{1}/_{2}$ teaspoon grated lemon zest
60 ml (2 fl oz/$^{1}/_{4}$ cup) lemon juice

1. Preheat the oven to 180°C (350°F/Gas 4). Lightly grease a deep 20 cm (8 inch) round cake tin and line with baking paper.

2. Sift the flour into a large bowl and add the coconut, lemon zest, sugar, butter, eggs and milk. Mix well with a wooden spoon until smooth.

3. Pour into the prepared tin and smooth the surface. Bake for 40 minutes, or until a skewer comes out clean when inserted into the centre of the cake. Leave the cake in the tin for 5 minutes before turning out onto a wire rack to cool completely.

4. To make the coconut icing, combine the icing sugar and coconut in a bowl, then add the lemon zest and enough lemon juice to make a stiff but spreadable icing. Spread the icing over the cold cake.

Panforte

Makes 1

110 g (3³/4 oz/³/4 cup) hazelnuts
110 g (3³/4 oz/³/4 cup) almonds
125 g (4¹/2 oz/²/3 cup) candied mixed peel, chopped
100 g (3¹/2 oz/¹/2 cup) glacé (candied) pineapple, chopped
grated zest of 1 lemon
75 g (2¹/2 oz/²/3 cup) plain (all-purpose) flour
1 teaspoon ground cinnamon
¹/4 teaspoon ground coriander
¹/4 teaspoon ground cloves
¹/4 teaspoon grated nutmeg
pinch of white pepper
150 g (5¹/2 oz/²/3 cup) sugar
80 g (2³/4 oz/¹/4 cup) honey
50 g (1³/4 oz) unsalted butter
icing (confectioners') sugar, to dust

1   Line a 20 cm (8 inch) spring-form cake tin with baking paper and
    grease well with butter.

2   Toast the nuts under a hot grill (broiler), turning them so they brown
    on all sides, then leave to cool. Put the nuts in a bowl with the mixed
    peel, pineapple, lemon zest, flour and spices and toss together.
    Preheat the oven to 150°C (300°F/Gas 2).

3   Put the sugar, honey and butter in a saucepan and melt them
    together. Cook the syrup until it reaches 118°C (245°F) on a sugar
    thermometer, or when a little of it dropped into cold water forms
    a firm ball when moulded between your fingers.

4 Pour the syrup into the nut mixture and mix well, working fast before it stiffens too much. Pour straight into the prepared tin, smooth the surface and bake for 35 minutes. (Unlike other cakes, this cake will neither firm up as it cooks nor colour at all, so you need to time it carefully.)

5 Cool in the tin until the cake firms up enough to remove the side of the tin. Peel off the paper and leave to cool completely. Dust the top with icing sugar.

Blueberry Muffins

Makes 12

375 g (13 oz/3 cups) plain (all-purpose) flour
1 tablespoon baking powder
165 g (5³/4 oz/3/4 cup firmly packed) soft brown sugar
125 g (4¹/2 oz) unsalted butter, melted
2 eggs, lightly beaten
250 ml (9 fl oz/1 cup) milk
185 g (6¹/2 oz/1¹/4 cups) fresh or thawed frozen blueberries

1 Preheat the oven to 210°C (415°F/Gas 6–7). Grease or brush two trays of six (or one tray of 12) 125 ml (4 fl oz/¹/2 cup) muffin holes with melted butter or oil.

2 Sift the flour and baking powder into a large bowl. Stir in the sugar and make a well in the centre.

3 Add the combined butter, eggs and milk all at once, and fold until just combined. Do not overmix—the batter should look quite lumpy.

4 Fold in the blueberries. Spoon the batter into the prepared tin. Bake for 20 minutes, or until golden brown. Cool on a wire rack.

 Make sure to completely cool the melted butter before adding it to the muffin mixture. Overmixing will make the muffins tough.

Caramel Rhubarb Cake

Makes 1

230 g (8¹/2 oz/1 cup) caster (superfine) sugar
250 g (9 oz/2 cups) chopped rhubarb
1 small granny smith apple, peeled, cored and sliced
2 eggs
40 g (1¹/2 oz/¹/3 cup) icing (confectioners') sugar
¹/2 teaspoon natural vanilla extract
100 g (3¹/2 oz) butter, melted and cooled
125 g (4¹/2 oz/1 cup) self-raising flour

1   Preheat the oven to 180°C (350°F/Gas 4). Grease the base and
    side of a deep 20 cm (8 inch) round cake tin and line the base with
    baking paper.

2   Put the sugar in a saucepan with 80 ml (2¹/2 fl oz/¹/3 cup) water and
    heat gently, shaking occasionally, until dissolved. Increase the heat
    and cook until a pale caramel colour—it will turn a deeper colour in
    the oven. Pour into the prepared tin and then press the rhubarb and
    apple into the caramel.

3   Beat the eggs, icing sugar and vanilla extract until frothy. Fold in the
    butter. Sift the flour over the top and stir (the mixture will be soft).
    Spoon gently over the fruit, being careful not to dislodge it.

4   Bake for 45 minutes, or until set on top. Run a knife around the side
    of the cake and turn out very carefully onto a wire rack or plate.
    Best served warm with clotted cream. If you don't turn the cake out
    straight away the caramel will cool and make it stick to the tin.

Lamingtons

Makes 16

185 g (6^1/$_2$ oz/1^1/$_2$ cups) self-raising flour
40 g (1^1/$_2$ oz/^{1}/$_3$ cup) cornflour (cornstarch)
185 g (6^1/$_2$ oz) unsalted butter, softened
250 g (9 oz/1 heaped cup) caster (superfine) sugar
2 teaspoons natural vanilla extract
3 eggs, lightly beaten
125 ml (4 fl oz/^{1}/$_2$ cup) milk
185 ml (6^1/$_2$ fl oz/^{3}/$_4$ cup) thickened (whipping) cream

ICING
500 g (1 lb 2 oz/4 cups) icing (confectioners') sugar
40 g (1^1/$_2$ oz/^{1}/$_3$ cup) unsweetened cocoa powder
30 g (1 oz) unsalted butter, melted
170 ml (5^1/$_2$ fl oz/^{2}/$_3$ cup) milk
270 g (9^1/$_2$ oz/3 cups) desiccated coconut

1 Preheat the oven to 180°C (350°F/Gas 4). Lightly grease a shallow 23 cm (9 inch) square cake tin and line the base and sides with baking paper.

2 Sift the flour and cornflour into a large bowl. Add the butter, sugar, vanilla extract, eggs and milk. Using electric beaters, beat on low speed for 1 minute, or until the ingredients are just moistened. Increase the speed to high and beat for 3 minutes, or until free of lumps and increased in volume. Pour into the prepared tin and smooth the surface. Bake for 50–55 minutes, or until a skewer comes out clean when inserted into the centre of the cake. Leave in the tin for 3 minutes before turning out onto a wire rack to cool.

3 Using a serrated knife, trim the top of the cake until flat. Trim the crusts from the sides, then cut the cake in half horizontally. Using electric beaters, beat the cream in a small bowl until stiff peaks form. Place the first layer of cake on a board and spread it evenly with cream. Place the remaining cake layer on top. Cut the cake into 16 squares.

4 To make the icing, sift the icing sugar and cocoa into a heatproof bowl and add the butter and milk. Stand the bowl over a saucepan of simmering water, stirring, or until the icing is smooth and glossy, then remove from the heat. Place 90 g (3¼ oz/1 cup) of the coconut on a sheet of baking paper. Using two forks, roll a piece of cake in chocolate icing, then hold the cake over a bowl and allow the excess to drain off. (Add 1 tablespoon boiling water to the icing if it seems too thick.) Roll the cake in coconut, then place on a wire rack. Repeat with the remaining pieces of cake, adding extra coconut for rolling as needed.

 If you cook the cake a day ahead, it will be easier to cut and won't crumble as much. Lamingtons are not necessarily cream-filled, so if you prefer, you can ice unfilled squares of cake.

Almond Friands

Makes 10

160 g (5¹/2 oz) unsalted butter
90 g (3¹/4 oz/1 cup) flaked almonds
40 g (1¹/2 oz/¹/3 cup) plain (all-purpose) flour
165 g (5³/4 oz/1¹/3 cups) icing (confectioners') sugar
5 egg whites
icing (confectioners') sugar, extra, to dust

1 Preheat the oven to 210°C (415°F/Gas 6–7). Lightly grease ten 125 ml (4 fl oz/¹/2 cup) friand tins.

2 Melt the butter in a small saucepan over medium heat, then cook for 3–4 minutes, or until the butter turns deep golden. Strain to remove any residue (the colour will deepen on standing). Remove from the heat and set aside to cool until just lukewarm.

3 Place the flaked almonds in a food processor and process until finely ground. Transfer to a bowl and sift the flour and icing sugar into the same bowl.

4 Place the egg whites in a separate bowl and lightly whisk with a fork until just combined. Add the butter to the flour mixture along with the egg whites. Mix gently with a metal spoon until well combined.

5 Spoon some mixture into each friand tin to fill to three-quarters. Place the tins on a baking tray and bake in the centre of the oven for 10 minutes, then reduce the oven temperature to 180°C (350°F/Gas 4) and bake for another 5 minutes, or until a skewer comes out clean when inserted into the centre of a friand.

6   Remove from the oven and leave to cool in the tins for 5 minutes
    before turning out onto a wire rack to cool completely. Dust with
    icing sugar before serving.

 To make lemon friands, add 2 teaspoons
    grated lemon zest to the flour and sugar
    mixture and proceed as above.

Mango Cakes with Lime Syrup

Makes 4 small cakes

425 g (15 oz/2 heaped cups) tinned mango slices in syrup, drained

90 g (3^1/4 oz) unsalted butter, softened

185 g (6^1/2 oz/heaped ^{3}/4 cup) caster (superfine) sugar

2 eggs, lightly beaten

60 g (2^1/4 oz/^{1}/2 cup) self-raising flour

2 tablespoons ground almonds

2 tablespoons coconut milk

2 tablespoons lime juice

1 Preheat the oven to 200°C (400°F/Gas 6). Grease four 250 ml
   (9 fl oz/1 cup) muffin holes and line with mango slices.

2 Cream the butter and 125 g (4^1/2 oz/^{1}/2 cup) of the sugar in a bowl
   with electric beaters until light and fluffy. Gradually add the eggs,
   beating well after each addition. Fold in the sifted flour, then add the
   almonds and coconut milk.

3 Spoon into the muffin holes. Bake for 25 minutes, or until a skewer
   comes out clean when inserted into the centre of the cakes.

4 To make the syrup, place the lime juice, the remaining sugar and
   125 ml (4 fl oz/^{1}/2 cup) water in a small saucepan and stir over
   low heat until the sugar has dissolved. Increase the heat and simmer
   for 10 minutes. Pierce holes in each cake with a skewer. Drizzle the
   syrup over the top and allow to stand for 5 minutes to soak up the
   liquid. Turn out and serve.

Rum and Raisin Cake

Makes 1

160 g (5³/4 oz/1¹/4 cups) raisins
60 ml (2 fl oz/¹/4 cup) dark rum
185 g (6¹/2 oz/1¹/2 cups) self-raising flour
150 g (5¹/2 oz) unsalted butter, cubed
140 g (5 oz/³/4 cup) soft brown sugar
3 eggs, lightly beaten
ice cream, to serve

1 Preheat the oven to 180°C (350°F/Gas 4). Grease a deep 20 cm (8 inch) round cake tin and line the base with baking paper.

2 Soak the raisins in the rum in a small bowl for 10 minutes. Sift the flour into a large bowl and make a well in the centre.

3 Melt the butter and sugar in a small saucepan over low heat, stirring until the sugar has dissolved. Remove from the heat. Combine with the rum and raisin mixture and add to the flour with the egg. Stir with a wooden spoon until combined—do not overbeat. Spoon the mixture into the prepared tin and smooth the surface.

4 Bake for 40 minutes, or until a skewer comes out clean when inserted into the centre of the cake. Serve with ice cream.

A cake is quite fragile when removed from the oven, so always leave it in the tin for the recommended time before turning out. If the cake is stuck to the tin, gently run a flat-bladed knife around the side to release it. Remove the lining paper immediately.

Lumberjack Cake

Makes 1

200 g (7 oz/1¼ cups) fresh dates, pitted and chopped
1 teaspoon bicarbonate of soda (baking soda)
125 g (4½ oz) unsalted butter, softened
250 g (9 oz/1 heaped cup) caster (superfine) sugar
1 egg
1 teaspoon natural vanilla extract
2 granny smith apples, peeled, cored and grated
125 g (4½ oz/1 cup) plain (all-purpose) flour
60 g (2¼ oz/½ cup) self-raising flour
icing (confectioners') sugar, optional, to dust

TOPPING
75 g (2½ oz) unsalted butter
95 g (3¼ oz/½ cup) soft brown sugar
80 ml (2½ fl oz/⅓ cup) milk
60 g (2¼ oz/1 cup) shredded coconut

1 Preheat the oven to 180°C (350°F/Gas 4). Grease a 20 cm (8 inch)
   round spring-form cake tin and line the base with baking paper.

2 Put the dates in a small saucepan with 250 ml (9 fl oz/1 cup) water
   and bring to the boil. Stir in the bicarbonate of soda, then remove
   from the heat. Set aside until just warm.

3 Cream the butter and sugar in a small bowl with electric beaters until
   light and fluffy. Add the egg and vanilla extract and beat until
   combined. Stir in the date mixture and the apple, then fold in the
   sifted flours until just combined and almost smooth. Spoon into
   the prepared tin and smooth the surface. Bake for 40 minutes.

4   Meanwhile, combine all the topping ingredients in a small saucepan and stir over low heat until the butter has melted and the ingredients are well combined. Remove the cake from the oven and carefully spread the topping over the cake. Return the cake to the oven for 20–30 minutes, or until the topping is golden and the cake is cooked through.

5   Remove from the oven and leave in the tin to cool completely, then turn out carefully and place, topping side up, on a serving plate. The cake can be dusted with icing sugar just before serving.

Marble Cake

Makes 1

1 vanilla bean or 1 teaspoon natural vanilla extract
185 g (6½ oz) unsalted butter, cubed
230 g (8 oz/1 cup) caster (superfine) sugar
3 eggs
280 g (10 oz/2¼ cups) self-raising flour
185 ml (6½ fl oz/¾ cup) milk
2 tablespoons unsweetened cocoa powder
1½ tablespoons warm milk, extra

1   Preheat the oven to 200°C (400°F/Gas 6). Lightly grease a 25 x 11 x 7.5 cm (10 x 4¼ x 3 inch) loaf (bar) tin and line with baking paper.

2   If using the vanilla bean, split it down the middle and scrape out the seeds. Put the seeds (or vanilla extract) in a bowl with the butter and sugar and, using electric beaters, cream the mixture until light and fluffy. Add the eggs one at a time, beating well after each addition.

3   Sift the flour, then fold it into the creamed mixture alternately with the milk until combined. Divide the mixture in half and put the second half into another bowl.

4   Combine the cocoa powder and warm milk in a small bowl and stir until smooth, then add to one half of the cake mixture, stirring to combine well. Spoon the two mixtures into the prepared tin in alternate spoonfuls. Using a metal skewer, cut through the mixture four times to create a marble effect.

5   Bake for 50–60 minutes, or until a skewer inserted into the centre of the cake comes out clean. Leave in the tin for 5 minutes before turning out onto a wire rack to cool.

Orange Poppy Seed Cake with Citrus Icing

Makes 1

50 g (1³/4 oz/¹/3 cup) poppy seeds
185 ml (6 fl oz/³/4 cup) warm milk
250 g (9 oz/1 heaped cup) caster (superfine) sugar
3 eggs
250 g (9 oz/2 cups) self-raising flour, sifted
210 g (7¹/2 oz) unsalted butter, softened
1¹/2 tablespoons finely grated orange zest
250 g (9 oz/2 cups) icing (confectioners') sugar
3 tablespoons boiling water
thick (double/heavy) cream, to serve

1   Preheat the oven to 180°C (350°F/Gas 4). Lightly grease a 23 cm (9 inch) fluted cake tin. Combine the poppy seeds and milk in a bowl and set aside for at least 15 minutes.

2   Place the caster sugar, eggs, flour, 185 g (6¹/2 oz) of the butter and 3 teaspoons of the orange zest in a large bowl. Add the poppy seed mixture and beat with electric beaters on low speed until combined. Increase the speed to medium and beat for 3 minutes, or until thick and pale. Pour the mixture evenly into the prepared tin.

3   Bake for 50 minutes, or until a skewer comes out clean when inserted into the centre of the cake. Leave in the tin for 5 minutes, then turn out onto a wire rack.

4   To make the icing, melt the remaining butter, then mix in a bowl with the icing sugar, remaining orange zest and 3 tablespoons boiling water. Spread over the warm cake and serve with cream.

Madeira Cake

Makes 1

185 g (6¹/2 oz) unsalted butter, softened
185 g (6¹/2 oz/heaped ³/4 cup) caster (superfine) sugar
3 eggs, lightly beaten
2 teaspoons finely grated orange or lemon zest
155 g (5¹/2 oz/1¹/4 cups) self-raising flour
125 g (4¹/2 oz/1 cup) plain (all-purpose) flour
2 tablespoons milk

1 Preheat the oven to 160°C (315°F/Gas 2–3). Lightly grease a
   20 x 10 x 7 cm (8 x 4 x 2³/4 inch) loaf (bar) tin and line the base
   and side with baking paper.

2 Cream the butter and sugar in a small bowl with electric beaters
   until light and fluffy. Add the eggs gradually, beating thoroughly
   after each addition. Add the zest and beat until combined. Transfer
   to a large bowl. Using a metal spoon, fold in the sifted flours and
   milk. Stir until smooth.

3 Spoon into the prepared tin and smooth the surface. Bake for
   50 minutes, or until a skewer comes out clean when inserted into the
   centre of the cake. Cool in the tin for 10 minutes before turning out
   onto a wire rack to cool completely.

This cake keeps well in an airtight container
for up to 1 week.

Pumpkin Fruitcake

Makes 1

250 g (9 oz/1²/₃ cups) pumpkin (winter squash), peeled and cut into
    small pieces

125 g (4¹/₂ oz) unsalted butter, softened

140 g (5 oz/³/₄ cup) soft brown sugar

2 tablespoons golden syrup (or substitute honey, maple syrup
    or treacle)

2 eggs, lightly beaten

250 g (9 oz/2 cups) self-raising flour, sifted

200 g (7 oz/1 heaped cup) mixed dried fruit

2 tablespoons chopped glacé (candied) ginger

1 Preheat the oven to 150°C (300°F/Gas 2). Grease a deep 20 cm
(8 inch) round cake tin and line the base and side with baking paper.

2 Steam the pumpkin for 10 minutes, or until cooked through. Mash
with a potato masher or a fork until smooth. Measure 200 g (7 oz/
1¹/₂ cups) and set aside until ready to use.

3 Cream the butter and sugar with electric beaters until pale and fluffy.
Add the golden syrup and beat well. Gradually add the eggs, beating
well after each addition. Fold in the pumpkin until combined.
Combine the flour, dried fruit and ginger, then fold into the butter
mixture with a metal spoon until combined. Spoon the mixture into
the prepared tin and smooth the surface.

4 Bake for 1 hour 40 minutes, or until a skewer comes out clean when
inserted into the centre of the cake. Cool in the tin for 20 minutes
before turning out onto a wire rack.

Hawaiian Macadamia Cake

Makes 1

375 g (13 oz/3 cups) self-raising flour

1 teaspoon ground cinnamon

375 g (13 oz/1²/₃ cups) caster (superfine) sugar

90 g (3¹/₄ oz/1 cup) desiccated coconut

5 eggs, lightly beaten

440 g (1 lb) tinned crushed pineapple in syrup

375 ml (13 fl oz/1¹/₂ cups) vegetable oil

100 g (3¹/₂ oz/³/₄ cup) macadamia nuts, chopped

LEMON CREAM CHEESE ICING

60 g (2¹/₄ oz/¹/₄ cup) cream cheese, softened

30 g (1 oz) unsalted butter, softened

1 tablespoon lemon juice

185 g (6¹/₂ oz/1¹/₂ cups) icing (confectioners') sugar, sifted

1　Preheat the oven to 180°C (350°F/Gas 4). Grease a deep 23 cm (9 inch) round cake tin. Line the base and side with two sheets of baking paper, cutting it to sit 2–3 cm (³/₄–1¹/₄ inch) above the side of the tin.

2　Sift the flour and cinnamon into a bowl, add the sugar and coconut and stir to combine. Add the eggs, pineapple and oil and mix well. Stir in the macadamia nuts. Spoon the mixture into the prepared tin and smooth the surface. Bake for 1 hour 15 minutes, or until a skewer comes out clean when inserted into the centre of the cake. Leave in the tin for 30 minutes before turning out onto a wire rack.

3　To make the lemon cream cheese icing, beat the cream cheese and butter in a small bowl. Add the lemon juice and icing sugar and beat until smooth. Spread over the cooled cake.

Tiramisu

Makes 1 large dish

5 eggs, separated
180 g (6½ oz/heaped ¾ cup) caster (superfine) sugar
300 g (10½ oz) mascarpone cheese
250 ml (9 fl oz/1 cup) cold, strong espresso coffee
3 tablespoons brandy
36 small savoiardi (lady fingers)
80 g (2¾ oz/⅔ cup) dark chocolate, finely grated

1   Whisk the egg yolks with the sugar until the sugar has dissolved and the mixture is light and fluffy and leaves a ribbon trail when dropped from the whisk. Add the mascarpone and beat until smooth.

2   Whisk the egg whites in a clean dry glass bowl, using a wire whisk or hand beaters, until soft peaks form. Fold into the mascarpone mixture.

3   Pour the coffee into a shallow dish and add the brandy. Dip enough savoiardi to cover the base of a 25 cm (10 inch) square dish into the coffee mixture. The savoiardi should be fairly well soaked but not so much that they break up. Arrange the savoiardi in one tightly packed layer in the base of the dish.

4   Spread half the mascarpone mixture over the layer of savoiardi. Add another layer of soaked savoiardi and then another layer of mascarpone, smoothing the top layer neatly. To serve, sprinkle with the grated chocolate.

Sacher Torte

Makes 1

125 g (4½ oz/1 cup) plain (all-purpose) flour
30 g (1 oz/¼ cup) unsweetened cocoa powder
250 g (9 oz/1 heaped cup) caster (superfine) sugar
100 g (3½ oz) unsalted butter
80 g (2¾ oz/¼ cup) strawberry jam
4 eggs, separated

GANACHE TOPPING
170 ml (5½ fl oz/⅔ cup) pouring (whipping) cream
90 g (3¼ oz/⅓ cup) caster (superfine) sugar
200 g (7 oz/1⅓ cups) chopped dark chocolate

1 Preheat the oven to 180°C (350°F/Gas 4). Lightly grease a 20 cm (8 inch) round cake tin and line the base and side with baking paper.

2 Sift the flour and cocoa into a bowl and make a well in the centre. Combine the sugar, butter and half the jam in a saucepan. Stir over low heat until the butter has melted and the sugar has dissolved. Add to the flour with the lightly beaten egg yolks and stir until just combined.

3 Beat the egg whites in a small bowl with electric beaters until soft peaks form. Stir one-third of the egg white into the cake mixture, then fold in the rest in two batches. Pour into the prepared tin and smooth the surface. Bake for 40–45 minutes, or until a skewer comes out clean when inserted into the centre of the cake. Leave in the tin for 15 minutes before turning out onto a wire rack to cool.

4 To make the ganache topping, stir the cream, sugar and chocolate in a small saucepan over low heat until melted and smooth.

5   Trim the top of the cake so that it is flat, then turn it upside down on
    a wire rack over a tray. Melt the remaining jam and brush it over the
    cake. Pour the topping over the cake and tap the tray to flatten the
    surface. Place the remaining mixture in a piping bag and pipe 'Sacher'
    on the top of the cake (see note).

Vienna's most famous torte was created in
1832 by Franz Sacher, a pastry cook from a
famous family of restaurateurs and hoteliers.
It is usually served with lashings of whipped
cream and it is traditional to write the word
'Sacher' in chocolate across the top.

Hummingbird Cake

Makes 1

2 ripe bananas, mashed
125 g (4^1/$_2$ oz/^{1}/$_2$ cup) drained tinned crushed pineapple
310 g (11 oz/1^1/$_3$ cups) caster (superfine) sugar
210 g (7^1/$_2$ oz/1^2/$_3$ cups) self-raising flour
2 teaspoons ground cinnamon or mixed (pumpkin pie) spice
170 ml (5^1/$_2$ fl oz/^{2}/$_3$ cup) oil
60 ml (2 fl oz/^{1}/$_4$ cup) pineapple juice
2 eggs

ICING
60 g (2^1/$_4$ oz) unsalted butter, softened
125 g (4^1/$_2$ oz/^{1}/$_2$ cup) cream cheese, softened
185 g (6^1/$_2$ oz/1^1/$_2$ cups) icing (confectioners') sugar
1–2 teaspoons lemon juice

1 Preheat the oven to 180°C (350°F/Gas 4). Lightly grease a 20 cm (8 inch) square cake tin and line the base and side with baking paper.

2 Place the banana, pineapple and sugar in a large bowl. Add the sifted flour and cinnamon or mixed spice. Stir together with a wooden spoon until well combined.

3 Whisk together the oil, pineapple juice and eggs in a jug. Pour onto the banana mixture and stir until combined and smooth.

4 Spoon into the tin and smooth the surface. Bake for 1 hour, or until a skewer comes out clean when inserted into the centre of the cake. Leave in the tin for 15 minutes before turning out onto a wire rack to cool.

5   To make the icing, beat the butter and cream cheese with electric beaters until smooth. Gradually add the icing sugar alternately with the lemon juice. Beat until thick and creamy.

6   Spread the icing thickly over the top of the cooled cake, or thinly over the top and side.

 If you are unable to buy tinned crushed pineapple, use tinned pineapple rings, drained and chopped very finely. Buy the fruit in natural juice rather than syrup; reserve the juice to use in the recipe.

passionfruit melting moments scottish shor

Cookies

apple and cinnamon oatcakes florentines

Anzac Biscuits

Makes 26

125 g (4½ oz/1 cup) plain (all-purpose) flour
160 g (5¾ oz/¾ cup) sugar
100 g (3½ oz/1 cup) rolled (porridge) oats
90 g (3¼ oz/1 cup) desiccated coconut
125 g (4½ oz) unsalted butter, cubed
90 g (3¼ oz/¼ cup) golden syrup or maple syrup
½ teaspoon bicarbonate of soda (baking soda)
1 tablespoon boiling water

1 Preheat the oven to 180°C (350°F/Gas 4). Line two baking trays with baking paper.

2 Sift the flour into a large bowl. Add the sugar, oats and coconut; mix together and make a well in the centre.

3 Put the butter and golden syrup together in a small saucepan and stir over low heat until the butter has melted and the mixture is smooth. Remove from the heat.

4 Dissolve the bicarbonate of soda in the boiling water and immediately add to the butter mixture. It will foam up instantly. Pour into the well in the dry ingredients and stir with a wooden spoon until well combined.

5 Drop level tablespoons of mixture onto the prepared trays, allowing room for spreading. Gently flatten each biscuit with your fingertips. Bake for 20 minutes, or until just browned. Leave on the trays to cool slightly, then transfer to a wire rack to cool completely. Store in an airtight container.

Chocolate Crunchies

Makes 25

150 g (5^1/$_2$ oz) unsalted butter, softened
60 g (2^1/$_4$ oz/^{1}/$_3$ cup) soft brown sugar
1 egg, lightly beaten
1 teaspoon natural vanilla extract
125 g (4^1/$_2$ oz/1 cup) plain (all-purpose) flour
2 tablespoons unsweetened cocoa powder
30 g (1 oz/^{1}/$_3$ cup) desiccated coconut
45 g (1^1/$_2$ oz/1 cup) lightly crushed cornflakes
90 g (3^1/$_4$ oz/^{2}/$_3$ cup) dark chocolate chips

1 Preheat the oven to 180°C (350°F/Gas 4). Line two baking trays with baking paper.

2 Cream the butter and sugar in a large bowl with electric beaters until light and fluffy. Add the egg and vanilla extract and beat thoroughly.

3 Add the sifted flour and cocoa to the bowl with the coconut and cornflakes. Stir with a metal spoon until the ingredients are just combined.

4 Drop level tablespoons of mixture onto the prepared trays, allowing room for spreading. Bake for 20 minutes, or until lightly browned, then leave on the trays to cool completely.

5 Place the chocolate chips in a small heatproof bowl. Bring a saucepan of water to the boil, then remove from the heat. Sit the bowl over the pan, making sure the base of the bowl does not touch the water. Stir until the chocolate has melted and the mixture is smooth. Spread the cookie thickly with chocolate and allow to set.

Passionfruit Melting Moments

Makes 14

250 g (9 oz) unsalted butter, softened

40 g (1½ oz/⅓ cup) icing (confectioners') sugar

1 teaspoon natural vanilla extract

185 g (6½ oz/1½ cups) self-raising flour

60 g (2¼ oz/½ cup) custard powder (instant vanilla pudding mix)

PASSIONFRUIT FILLING

60 g (2¼ oz) unsalted butter

60 g (2¼ oz/½ cup) icing (confectioners') sugar

1½ tablespoons passionfruit pulp

1 Preheat the oven to 180°C (350°F/Gas 4). Line two baking trays with baking paper.

2 Cream the butter and icing sugar in a bowl with electric beaters until light and fluffy, then beat in the vanilla extract. Sift in the flour and custard powder and mix with a knife, using a cutting motion, to form a soft dough.

3 Shape level tablespoons of dough into balls (you should have 28) and place on the prepared trays, leaving room for spreading. Flatten slightly with a floured fork. Bake for 20 minutes, or until light golden. Cool slightly on the trays before transferring to a wire rack to cool completely.

4 To make the passionfruit filling, cream the butter and sugar in a bowl with electric beaters until light and fluffy, then beat in the passionfruit pulp. Use to sandwich the cookie together. Leave to firm before serving.

Cocoa Sesame Crunch

Makes 33

90 g (3^1/$_4$ oz/^{3}/$_4$ cup) plain (all-purpose) flour

90 g (3^1/$_4$ oz/^{1}/$_4$ cup) unsweetened cocoa powder

75 g (2^1/$_2$ oz/^{3}/$_4$ cup) rolled (porridge) oats

155 g (5^1/$_2$ oz/1 cup) sesame seeds

170 g (5^3/$_4$ oz/^{3}/$_4$ cup) caster (superfine) sugar

100 g (3^1/$_2$ oz) unsalted butter

2 tablespoons golden syrup or maple syrup

1 tablespoon boiling water

1 teaspoon bicarbonate of soda (baking soda)

185 g (6^1/$_2$ oz/1^1/$_4$ cups) milk chocolate melts (buttons), melted

1 Preheat the oven to 160°C (315°F/Gas 2–3). Line two baking trays with baking paper.

2 Sift the flour and cocoa into a large bowl. Add the oats, sesame seeds and sugar; make a well in the centre.

3 Combine the butter and golden syrup in a saucepan. Stir over low heat until the butter is melted and the mixture is smooth, then remove from heat. Pour the boiling water into a bowl and add the bicarbonate of soda. Stir until dissolved. Add to the golden syrup mixture. Using a metal spoon, fold the mixture into the dry ingredients. Stir until well combined.

4 Drop 3 level tablespoons of mixture at a time onto the prepared trays, allowing room for spreading. Flatten each one slightly. Bake for 12 minutes; cool cookies on the trays for 5 minutes. Transfer to a wire rack to cool completely. Spread approximately one teaspoon of chocolate into 3 cm (1^1/$_4$ inch) round in the centre of each cookie.

Scottish Shortbread

Makes 16 pieces

250 g (9 oz) unsalted butter, softened
160 g (5¾ oz/¾ cup) caster (superfine) sugar
210 g (7½ oz/1⅔ cups) plain (all-purpose) flour
90 g (3¼ oz/½ cup) rice flour
1 teaspoon sugar

1   Preheat the oven to 160°C (315°F/Gas 2–3). Brush a 28 cm (11¼ inch) round pizza tray with melted butter or oil and line with baking paper.

2   Cream the butter and sugar with electric beaters in a small bowl until light and fluffy. Transfer to a large bowl and add the sifted flours. Mix to a soft dough with a flat-bladed knife. Lift the dough onto a lightly floured work surface and knead for 30 seconds, or until the mixture is smooth.

3   Transfer to the pizza tray and press into a 25 cm (10 inch) round (the tray must be larger than the uncooked shortbread as the mixture will spread during cooking). Pinch and flute around the edge with your fingers to decorate. Prick the surface lightly with a fork and mark into 16 segments with a sharp knife. Sprinkle with the sugar and bake on the middle shelf of the oven for 35 minutes, or until firm and lightly golden. Allow the shortbread to cool on the tray.

Almond Cinnamon Bites

Makes 45

200 g (7 oz/1^1/3 cups) blanched almonds
80 g (2^3/4 oz/^{1}/3 cup) caster (superfine) sugar
40 g (1^1/2 oz/^{1}/3 cup) icing (confectioners') sugar
3 teaspoons ground cinnamon
90 g (3^1/4 oz/^{3}/4 cup) plain (all-purpose) flour

VANILLA ICING
210 g (7^1/2 oz/1^2/3 cups) icing (confectioners') sugar
1 egg white, lightly beaten
^{1}/2 teaspoon natural vanilla extract

1 Preheat the oven to 150°C (300°F/Gas 2). Line two baking trays with baking paper.

2 Place the almonds, sugars, cinnamon and flour in a food processor. Using the pulse action, process for 30 seconds, or until the mixture is fine and crumbly. Add the egg whites and process for a further 30 seconds, or until a soft dough forms.

3 Turn the dough out onto a lightly floured surface. Knead for 1 minute, then shape into a ball. Roll between two sheets of plastic wrap to 5 mm (1/4 inch) thick. Cut into shapes, using a 4 cm (1^1/2 inch) plain or fluted biscuit/cookie cutter, and place on the prepared trays. Bake for 20 minutes, or until golden. Transfer to a wire rack to cool.

4 To make the vanilla icing, sift the icing sugar into a small bowl. Make a well in the centre, then add the egg white and vanilla extract. Beat constantly until all the icing sugar is incorporated and a firm paste is formed. Using a flat-bladed knife, spread over the cookies.

Choc-chip Cookies

Makes 16

125 g (4^1/$_2$ oz) unsalted butter
185 g (6^1/$_2$ oz/1 cup) soft brown sugar
1 teaspoon natural vanilla extract
1 egg, lightly beaten
1 tablespoon milk
215 g (7^3/$_4$ oz/1^3/$_4$ cups) plain (all-purpose) flour
1 teaspoon baking powder
250 g (9 oz/1^1/$_2$ cups) dark chocolate chips

1 Preheat the oven to 180°C (350°F/Gas 4). Line a large baking tray with baking paper.

2 Cream the butter and sugar with electric beaters in a large bowl until light and fluffy. Mix in the vanilla extract and gradually add the egg, beating well. Stir in the milk.

3 Sift the flour and baking powder into a large bowl, then fold into the butter and egg mixture. Stir in the chocolate chips.

4 Drop level tablespoons of mixture onto the baking tray, leaving about 4 cm (1^1/$_2$ inches) between each cookie, then lightly press with a floured fork. Bake for 15 minutes, or until light golden. Cool on a wire rack.

Peanut Butter Cookies

Makes 30

125 g (4^1/$_2$ oz/1 cup) plain (all-purpose) flour
60 g (2^1/$_4$ oz/^{1}/$_2$ cup) self-raising flour
100 g (3^1/$_2$ oz/1 cup) rolled (porridge) oats
125 g (4^1/$_2$ oz) unsalted butter
115 g (4 oz/^{1}/$_2$ cup) caster (superfine) sugar
115 g (4 oz/^{1}/$_3$ cup) honey
2 tablespoons peanut butter
160 g (5^3/$_4$ oz/1 cup) roasted unsalted peanuts, finely chopped

TOPPING
90 g (3^1/$_4$ oz/^{3}/$_4$ cup) icing (confectioners') sugar
25 g (1 oz) unsalted butter, softened

1   Preheat the oven to 180°C (350°F/Gas 4). Brush two baking trays with melted butter or oil.

2   Sift the flours into a large bowl and stir in the oats.

3   Combine the butter, sugar, honey and peanut butter in a saucepan and stir over medium heat until melted. Add to the flour mixture. Using a metal spoon, stir to just combine the ingredients.

4   Roll heaped teaspoons of mixture into balls. Arrange on the prepared trays, leaving room for spreading, and press lightly to flatten. Bake for 10 minutes, or until golden. Cool on the trays.

5   To make the topping, combine the icing sugar, butter and 1 tablespoon warm water in a small bowl. Stir until smooth. Dip the tops of the cookies into the topping, then into the chopped peanuts.

Choc-chestnut Creams

Makes 35

125 g (4¹/₂ oz/1 cup) plain (all-purpose) flour

1 teaspoon unsweetened cocoa powder

¹/₄ teaspoon ground cinnamon

50 g (1³/₄ oz) unsalted butter

80 g (2³/₄ oz/¹/₃ cup) caster (superfine) sugar

1 egg

200 g (7 oz/1¹/₃ cups) dark chocolate chips

1 tablespoon vegetable oil

50 g (1³/₄ oz/¹/₃ cup) white chocolate melts (buttons)

CHESTNUT CREAM FILLING

125 g (4¹/₂ oz/¹/₂ cup) cream cheese

60 g (2¹/₄ oz/¹/₄ cup) sweetened chestnut spread

1 Preheat the oven to 180°C (350°F/Gas 4). Line two baking trays with baking paper.

2 Place the flour, cocoa and cinnamon in a food processor and add the butter and sugar. Using the pulse action, process for 30 seconds, or until the mixture is fine and crumbly. Add the egg and process for a further 15 seconds, or until a soft dough forms.

3 Turn the dough out onto a lightly floured surface and knead for 1 minute, or until smooth. Roll the dough to 4 mm (¹/₈ inch) thick. Cut into 4 cm (1¹/₂ inch) rounds, using a fluted biscuit/cookie cutter. Place on the prepared trays. Bake for 12 minutes, or until light golden. Cool the cookies on the trays.

4   Place the chocolate chips in a small heatproof bowl. Stand the bowl over a saucepan of simmering water and stir until the chocolate is melted, then remove from the heat. Add the oil and beat until smooth. Cool slightly.

5   To make the chestnut cream filling, beat the cream cheese in a small bowl until light and creamy. Add the chestnut spread and beat for a further 1 minute, or until well combined. Spoon the filling into a piping bag fitted with a fluted 5 mm (1/4 inch) wide piping nozzle and pipe a swirl over each cookie. Dip each cookie into the melted chocolate, coating the filling and top of the cookie only. Place on a wire rack to set.

6   Gently melt the white chocolate melts and use to pipe fine swirly lines over each cookie.

Cinnamon Pecan Rounds

Makes 40

100 g (3¹/2 oz/²/3 cup) chopped dark chocolate
125 g (4¹/2 oz) unsalted butter
115 g (4 oz/¹/2 cup) caster (superfine) sugar
1 egg, lightly beaten
90 g (3¹/4 oz/³/4 cup) finely chopped pecans
40 g (1¹/2 oz/¹/3 cup) self-raising flour
85 g (3 oz/²/3 cup) plain (all-purpose) flour
2 teaspoons ground cinnamon
50 g (1³/4 oz/¹/2 cup) whole pecans, to decorate
1 tablespoon icing (confectioners') sugar, to dust

1   Preheat the oven to 180°C (350°F/Gas 4). Line two baking trays
    with baking paper.

2   Place the chocolate in a small heatproof bowl. Stand the bowl over a
    saucepan of simmering water. Stir until the chocolate is melted and
    smooth. Allow to cool but not to reset.

3   Using electric beaters, cream the butter and sugar in a small mixing
    bowl until light and fluffy. Add the egg gradually, beating thoroughly.
    Add the cooled melted chocolate and beat until combined.

4   Transfer the mixture to a large bowl and add the chopped pecans.
    Using a metal spoon, fold in the sifted flours and cinnamon.
    Stir until the ingredients are combined; do not overbeat.

5   Lightly roll 2 teaspoonsful of mixture at a time into oval shapes,
    place on the prepared trays and press a whole pecan onto each. Bake
    for 10 minutes. Transfer to a wire rack to cool. Dust with the sifted
    icing sugar.

Cornflake Cookies

Makes 30

125 g (4¹/₂ oz) unsalted butter
170 g (5³/₄ oz/³/₄ cup) sugar
2 eggs, lightly beaten
1 teaspoon natural vanilla extract
2 tablespoons currants
135 g (4³/₄ oz/1¹/₂ cups) desiccated coconut
¹/₂ teaspoon bicarbonate of soda (baking soda)
¹/₂ teaspoon baking powder
250 g (9 oz/2 cups) plain (all-purpose) flour
150 g (5¹/₂ oz/3 cups) cornflakes, lightly crushed

1   Preheat the oven to 180°C (350°F/Gas 4). Line a baking tray with
    baking paper.

2   Using electric beaters, cream the butter and sugar in a small
    mixing bowl until light and fluffy. Add the egg gradually, beating
    thoroughly after each addition. Add the vanilla extract and beat
    until combined.

3   Transfer to a large bowl, then add the currants and coconut. Using a
    metal spoon, fold in the sifted bicarbonate of soda, baking powder
    and flour. Stir until just combined and almost smooth. Drop level
    tablespoons of mixture onto the cornflakes and roll into balls. Arrange
    on the prepared tray, allowing room for spreading.

4   Bake for 20 minutes, or until crisp and golden. Transfer the cookies
    to a wire rack to cool. Store in an airtight container.

Digestives

Makes 16

125 g (4¹/₂ oz) unsalted butter, softened
60 g (2¹/₄ oz/¹/₃ cup) soft brown sugar
1 tablespoon liquid malt extract
1 egg, lightly beaten
125 g (4¹/₂ oz/1 cup) plain (all-purpose) flour
150 g (5¹/₂ oz/1 cup) wholemeal (whole-wheat) flour
35 g (1¹/₄ oz/¹/₂ cup) unprocessed bran
1 teaspoon baking powder

1   Line two baking trays with baking paper. Cream the butter, sugar and malt in a small bowl with electric beaters until light and fluffy. Gradually add the egg, beating well after each addition. Transfer to a large bowl.

2   Sift the flours, bran and baking powder into a small bowl, returning the husks to the bowl. Using a large metal spoon, fold the dry ingredients into the creamed mixture in three portions; mix to a firm dough. Cover and refrigerate for at least 1 hour.

3   Preheat the oven to 180°C (350°F/Gas 4). Roll out half the dough between two sheets of baking paper to 5 mm (¹/₄ inch) thick. Cut out rounds using a 7 cm (2³/₄ inch) plain cutter and place the rounds on the prepared trays. Repeat with the remaining dough and re-roll any scraps. Refrigerate for 20 minutes to firm.

4   Bake for 12 minutes, or until golden brown and firm. Leave on the trays to cool slightly before transferring to a wire rack to cool completely. When the cookies are cold, store in an airtight container.

Apple and Cinnamon Oatcakes

Makes 20

90 g (3¹/4 oz/1 cup) chopped dried apple
125 ml (4 fl oz/¹/2 cup) boiling water
125 g (4¹/2 oz) unsalted butter
95 g (3¹/4 oz/¹/2 cup) soft brown sugar
1 egg, lightly beaten
75 g (2¹/2 oz/³/4 cup) rolled (porridge) oats
25 g (1 oz/¹/4 cup) desiccated coconut
125 g (4¹/2 oz/1 cup) self-raising flour
1 tablespoon cinnamon sugar

1 Preheat the oven to 180°C (350°F/Gas 4). Brush two baking trays with melted butter or oil. Combine the dried apple and water in a small bowl and let stand for 5 minutes, or until all the water is absorbed.

2 Cream the butter and sugar in a small mixing bowl until light and fluffy. Add the egg and beat thoroughly.

3 Transfer the mixture to a large bowl, then add the oats, coconut, apple and sifted flour. Using a metal spoon, stir until just combined.

4 Drop heaped tablespoons of mixture onto the prepared trays, allowing room for spreading.

5 Sprinkle with the cinnamon sugar. Bake for 20 minutes, or until lightly golden. Transfer to wire racks to cool.

Flaked Almond Tuiles

Makes 22

85 g (3 oz/^{2}/$_3$ cup) plain (all-purpose) flour
115 g (4 oz/^{1}/$_2$ cup) caster (superfine) sugar
60 g (2^1/$_4$ oz) unsalted butter, melted
2 egg whites, lightly beaten
^{1}/$_4$ teaspoon natural almond extract
45 g (1^1/$_2$ oz/^{1}/$_2$ cup) toasted flaked almonds

1 Brush two baking trays with melted butter or oil, line with baking paper and grease the paper.

2 Sift the flour into a bowl and add the sugar. Make a well in the centre. Add the butter, egg whites and almond extract. Using a wooden spoon, stir until well combined. Cover with plastic wrap and rest for 2 hours.

3 Preheat the oven to 180°C (350°F/Gas 4). Drop 2 level tablespoons of mixture at a time onto the prepared trays. Spread the mixture to around 10–12 cm (4–4^1/$_2$ inches) in diameter. Sprinkle each round with flaked almonds.

4 Bake for 5 minutes, or until light golden. Remove from the oven and stand on the trays for 30 seconds. Carefully loosen and lift the cookies from the trays. Shape by gently pressing while still warm over a bottle or rolling pin.

Florentines

Makes 12

55 g (2 oz) unsalted butter

45 g (1¹/₂ oz/¹/₄ cup) soft brown sugar

2 teaspoons honey

25 g (1 oz/¹/₄ cup) flaked almonds, roughly chopped

2 tablespoons chopped dried apricots

2 tablespoons chopped glacé (candied) cherries

2 tablespoons mixed peel

40 g (1¹/₂ oz/¹/₃ cup) plain (all-purpose) flour, sifted

120 g (4¹/₄ oz/³/₄ cup) dark chocolate pieces

1 Preheat the oven to 180°C (350°F/Gas 4). Melt the butter, sugar and honey in a saucepan until the butter is melted and all the ingredients are combined. Remove from the heat and add the almonds, apricots, cherries, mixed peel and flour. Mix well to combine.

2 Grease and line two baking trays with baking paper. Place level tablespoons of mixture well apart on the trays. Shape and flatten into 5 cm (2 inch) rounds.

3 Bake for 10 minutes, or until lightly browned. Cool on the trays, then allow to cool completely on a wire rack.

4 To melt the chocolate, put the pieces in a heatproof bowl. Bring a saucepan of water to a simmer, remove from the heat and place the bowl over the pan. Stir the chocolate until melted. Spread the melted chocolate on the bottom of each florentine and, using a fork, make a wavy pattern on the chocolate before it sets. Let the chocolate set completely before serving.

Gingernuts

Makes 50

250 g (9 oz/2 cups) plain (all-purpose) flour
1/2 teaspoon bicarbonate of soda (baking soda)
1 tablespoon ground ginger
1/2 teaspoon mixed (pumpkin pie) spice
125 g (4 1/2 oz) unsalted butter, chopped
185 g (6 1/2 oz/1 cup) soft brown sugar
60 ml (2 fl oz/1/4 cup) boiling water
1 tablespoon golden syrup or maple syrup

1. Preheat the oven to 180°C (350°F/Gas 4). Line two baking trays with baking paper.

2. Sift the flour, bicarbonate of soda, ginger and mixed spice into a large bowl. Add the butter and sugar and rub into the flour with your fingertips until the mixture resembles fine breadcrumbs.

3. Pour the boiling water into a small heatproof jug, add the golden syrup and stir until dissolved. Add to the flour and mix to a soft dough with a flat-bladed knife.

4. Roll into balls using 2 heaped teaspoons of mixture at a time. Place on the prepared trays, allowing room for spreading, and flatten out slightly with your fingertips. Bake for 15 minutes, or until well coloured and firm. Cool on the trays for 10 minutes before transferring to a wire rack to cool completely. Repeat with the remaining mixture. When cold, store in an airtight jar.

Crackle Cookies

Makes 60

125 g (4¹/2 oz) unsalted butter, cubed and softened
370 g (13 oz/2 cups) soft brown sugar
1 teaspoon natural vanilla extract
2 eggs
60 g (2¹/4 oz/¹/3 cup) chopped dark chocolate, melted
80 ml (2¹/2 fl oz/¹/3 cup) milk
340 g (11³/4 oz/2³/4 cups) plain (all-purpose) flour
2 tablespoons unsweetened cocoa powder
2 teaspoons baking powder
¹/4 teaspoon mixed (pumpkin pie) spice
85 g (3 oz/²/3 cup) chopped pecans
icing (confectioners') sugar, to dust

1 Cream the butter, sugar and vanilla extract until light and fluffy. Beat in the eggs, one at a time. Stir the chocolate and milk into the butter mixture.

2 Sift the flour, cocoa, baking powder, mixed spice and a pinch of salt into the butter mixture and mix well. Stir the pecans through. Refrigerate for at least 3 hours, or overnight.

3 Preheat the oven to 180°C (350°F/Gas 4). Lightly grease two baking trays. Roll tablespoons of the mixture into balls and roll each in icing sugar to coat. Place well apart on the baking trays. Bake for 20–25 minutes, or until lightly browned. Leave for 3–4 minutes, then cool on a wire rack.

Graham Crackers

Makes 12

350 g (12 oz/2^1/$_3$ cups) wholemeal (whole-wheat) flour
60 g (2^1/$_4$ oz/^{1}/$_2$ cup) cornflour (cornstarch)
60 g (2^1/$_4$ oz/^{1}/$_4$ cup) caster (superfine) sugar
150 g (5^1/$_2$ oz) butter
185 ml (6 fl oz/^{3}/$_4$ cup) pouring (whipping) cream

1   Sift the flours into a bowl, stir in the sugar and ^{1}/$_2$ teaspoon salt. Rub in the butter with your fingertips until the mixture resembles breadcrumbs. Mix in the cream with a knife, using a cutting motion, to make a pliable dough.

2   Gather the dough together and shape into a disc. Wrap in plastic wrap and refrigerate for 30 minutes.

3   Preheat the oven to 200°C (400°F/Gas 6). Line two baking trays with baking paper.

4   Roll out the dough to a rectangle measuring 30 x 24 cm (12 x 9^1/$_2$ inches). Cut the dough into 12 rectangles with a pastry wheel or sharp knife. Place the rectangles on the baking trays, allowing a little room for spreading.

5   Bake for 7–10 minutes, or until firm and golden brown. Leave to cool on the trays for 2–3 minutes, then transfer to a wire rack to cool completely. When the crackers are cold, store in an airtight container.

The original Graham crackers were a flat, crisp cookie made with a coarser grind than wholemeal (whole-wheat) flour.

Jaffa Rings

Makes 45

180 g (6^1/2 oz) unsalted butter
115 g (4 oz/^{1}/2 cup) caster (superfine) sugar
1 egg, lightly beaten
1^1/2 teaspoons finely grated orange zest
50 g (1^3/4 oz/^{1}/3 cup) grated milk chocolate
125 g (4^1/2 oz/1 cup) self-raising flour
250 g (9 oz/2 cups) plain (all-purpose) flour
100 g (3^1/2 oz/^{2}/3 cup) milk chocolate melts (buttons)

1 Preheat the oven to 180°C (350°F/Gas 4). Line two baking trays with baking paper.

2 Using electric beaters, cream the butter, sugar and egg until light and fluffy. Add the zest and chocolate and beat until combined.

3 Transfer the mixture to a large bowl. Using a flat-bladed knife, fold in the sifted flours and mix to form a soft dough. Turn onto a lightly floured surface and knead for 30 seconds, or until the dough is smooth.

4 Roll 2 teaspoonsful of mixture at a time into small rectangular shapes. Continue rolling into lengths of 20 cm (8 inches). Carefully fold in half and twist, then form into a ring. Place on the prepared trays. Bake for 12 minutes and transfer to a wire rack to cool.

5 Place the chocolate melts in a small heatproof bowl. Stand the bowl over a saucepan of simmering water and stir until the chocolate is melted and smooth. Cool slightly. Dip the bases of the cookies into the melted chocolate. Stand on a wire rack to set.

Choc-hazelnut Scrolls

Makes 35

250 g (9 oz/2 cups) plain (all-purpose) flour
55 g (2 oz/1/2 cup) ground hazelnuts
100 g (31/2 oz) unsalted butter, chopped
115 g (4 oz/1/2 cup) caster (superfine) sugar
1 egg, lightly beaten
2 tablespoons iced water
60 g (21/4 oz/1/4 cup) chocolate hazelnut spread

1 Place the flour and ground hazelnuts in a food processor; add the butter and sugar. Using the pulse action, process for 30 seconds or until mixture is fine and crumbly. Add the combined egg and water, then process for a further 20 seconds, or until the mixture forms a dough. Turn out onto a lightly floured surface and knead for 30 seconds, or until smooth.

2 Roll the pastry out on a large sheet of baking paper, to a rectangle 25 x 35 cm (10 x 14 inches). Trim any uneven edges. Spread the dough evenly with hazelnut spread. Using the paper to lift the dough, roll it up from the long side in Swiss (jelly) roll style. Wrap tightly in baking paper and refrigerate for 30 minutes.

3 Preheat the oven to 180°C (350°F/Gas 4). Line two baking trays with baking paper. Cut the dough into 1 cm (1/2 inch) slices, wiping the blade of the knife between cuts. Place on prepared trays and bake for 15 minutes. Transfer to a wire rack to cool.

Jam Drops

Makes 32

80 g (2³/4 oz) unsalted butter
80 g (2³/4 oz/¹/3 cup) caster (superfine) sugar
2 tablespoons milk
¹/2 teaspoon natural vanilla extract
125 g (4¹/2 oz/1 cup) self-raising flour
40 g (1¹/2 oz/¹/3 cup) custard powder (instant vanilla pudding mix)
2 tablespoons raspberry jam

1 Preheat the oven to 180°C (350°F/Gas 4). Line two baking trays with baking paper.

2 Using electric beaters, cream the butter and sugar in a mixing bowl until light and fluffy. Add the milk and vanilla extract and beat until combined.

3 Add the sifted flour and custard powder; mix to form a soft dough. Roll two teaspoonsful of mixture at a time into balls and place on the prepared trays.

4 Make an indentation in each ball using the end of a wooden spoon. Fill each hole with ¹/4 teaspoon of jam. Bake for 15 minutes and transfer to a wire rack when cool.

Macadamia and White Chocolate Cookies

Makes about 25

170 g (6 oz/1 cup) macadamia nuts, lightly toasted

1 egg

140 g (5 oz/3/4 cup) soft brown sugar

2 tablespoons sugar

1 teaspoon natural vanilla extract

125 ml (4 fl oz/1/2 cup) oil

60 g (21/4 oz/1/2 cup) plain (all-purpose) flour

30 g (1 oz/1/4 cup) self-raising flour

1/4 teaspoon ground cinnamon

30 g (1 oz/1/2 cup) shredded coconut

130 g (43/4 oz/3/4 cup) white chocolate chips

1 Roughly chop the macadamia nuts and set them aside.

2 Using electric beaters, cream the egg and sugars in a bowl until light and fluffy. Add the vanilla extract and oil. Using a wooden spoon, stir in the sifted flours, cinnamon, coconut, macadamia nuts and chocolate chips, and mix well. Refrigerate for 30 minutes.

3 Preheat the oven to 180°C (350°F/Gas 4). Grease and line two baking trays. Form rounded tablespoons of the mixture into balls and place on the baking trays, pressing the mixture together with your fingertips if it is crumbly. Bake for 12–15 minutes, or until golden. Cool slightly on the trays, then transfer to a wire rack.

Golden Triangles

Makes 40

125 g (4¹/₂ oz) unsalted butter
2 tablespoons caster (superfine) sugar
2 tablespoons golden syrup or maple syrup
75 g (2¹/₂ oz/¹/₂ cup) currants
50 g (1³/₄ oz/¹/₂ cup) rolled (porridge) oats
90 g (3¹/₄ oz/³/₄ cup) plain (all-purpose) flour
45 g (1¹/₂ oz/¹/₄ cup) rice flour

1 Using electric beaters, cream the butter, sugar and golden syrup in a small bowl until light and fluffy. Transfer the mixture to a large bowl and add the currants and oats. Using a metal spoon, stir well. Add the sifted flours, then stir until combined.

2 Roll the mixture into a log shape, 20 cm (8 inches) long. Press the log into a triangular shape. Refrigerate for 30 minutes, or until firm.

3 Preheat oven to 180°C (350°F/Gas 4). Brush two baking trays with melted butter or oil. Cut the log into 6 mm (¹/₄ inch) slices. Place slices and place on the prepared trays. Bake for 10 minutes, or until lightly golden. Transfer to a wire rack to cool.

Marzipan Swirls

Makes 54

100 g (3 1/2 oz) unsalted butter
30 g (1 oz/1/4 cup) icing (confectioners') sugar
2 egg yolks
100 g (3 1/2 oz) ready-made marzipan, chopped
60 g (2 1/4 oz/1/2 cup) self-raising flour
60 g (2 1/4 oz/1/2 cup) plain (all-purpose) flour
icing (confectioners') sugar, extra, to dust

1 Preheat the oven to 180°C (350°F/Gas 4). Line two baking trays with baking paper.

2 Using electric beaters, cream the butter and icing sugar in a small bowl until light and fluffy. Add the egg yolks and beat for another 1 minute. Transfer the mixture to a large mixing bowl.

3 Place the chopped marzipan and the flours in a food processor. Process for 20–30 seconds, or until the mixture resembles fine crumbs. Using a metal spoon, fold the flour mixture into the butter mixture. Stir until smooth. Spoon the mixture into a piping bag fitted with a wide, fluted nozzle.

4 Pipe stars about 4 cm (1 1/2 inches) in diameter onto the prepared trays, about 3 cm (1 1/4 inches) apart to allow for spreading. Bake for 10–15 minutes, or until just golden. Leave the cookies on the tray for 5 minutes, then transfer to a wire rack to cool. Dust with icing sugar.

Pecan and Coffee Biscotti

Makes 40

215 g (7³/4 oz/1³/4 cups) plain (all-purpose) flour
1/2 teaspoon baking powder
160 g (5³/4 oz/²/3 cup) caster (superfine) sugar
60 g (2¹/4 oz) unsalted butter
2 eggs
1/2 teaspoon natural vanilla extract
2 tablespoons instant coffee granules
135 g (4³/4 oz/1¹/3 cups) pecans
1/2 teaspoon caster (superfine) sugar, extra

1   Preheat the oven to 180°C (350°F/Gas 4) and line two baking trays with baking paper. Put the sifted flour, baking powder, sugar and a pinch of salt in a food processor and mix for 1–2 seconds. Add the butter and mix until the mixture resembles fine breadcrumbs. Add the eggs and vanilla extract and process until smooth.

2   Transfer the dough to a well-floured surface and knead in the coffee and pecans. Divide into two equal portions and, using lightly floured hands, shape each into a log about 20 cm (8 inches) long. Place the logs on the baking trays and sprinkle with the extra sugar. Press the top of each log down gently to make an oval.

3   Bake for 35 minutes, or until golden. Remove and set aside to cool for 20 minutes. Reduce the oven temperature to 170°C (325°F/Gas 3).

4   Cut the logs into 1 cm (¹/2 inch) slices. Turn the baking paper over, then spread the biscotti well apart on the trays so that they do not touch. Return to the oven and bake for 30 minutes, or until they just begin to colour. Cool completely before storing in an airtight container.

Fortune Cookies

Makes 30

3 egg whites
60 g (2¼ oz/½ cup) icing (confectioners') sugar, sifted
45 g (1½ oz) unsalted butter, melted
60 g (2¼ oz/½ cup) plain (all-purpose) flour

1 Preheat the oven to 180°C (350°F/Gas 4). Lightly grease a baking tray. Draw three 8 cm (3¼ inch) circles on a sheet of baking paper, turn over and use to line the tray.

2 Place the egg whites in a clean, dry bowl and whisk until just frothy. Add the icing sugar and butter and stir until smooth. Add the flour, mix until smooth and leave for 15 minutes. Using a flat-bladed knife, spread 2 level teaspoons of mixture over each circle. Bake for 5 minutes, or until slightly brown around the edges.

3 Working quickly, remove from the trays by sliding a flat-bladed knife under each round. Place a written fortune message in each cookie. Fold in half, then in half again, over the edge of a bowl or a palette knife. Keep a tea (dish) towel handy to use when folding the cookies. The tray is hot and you need to work fast, so take care not to burn your hands. Cool on a wire rack. Cook the remaining mixture the same way.

 Make two or three fortune cookies at a time, otherwise they will harden too quickly and break when folding.

Chocolate Lemon Swirls

Makes 60

125 g (4½ oz) unsalted butter
85 g (3 oz/⅔ cup) icing (confectioners') sugar
1 egg, lightly beaten
2 teaspoons grated lemon zest
155 g (5½ oz/1¼ cups) plain (all-purpose) flour
30 g (1 oz/¼ cup) unsweetened cocoa powder
2 tablespoons finely chopped mixed peel

1 Preheat the oven to 180°C (350°F/Gas 4). Line two baking trays with baking paper.

2 Using electric beaters, cream the butter and sugar until light and fluffy. Add the egg and lemon zest and beat well until combined. Add the flour and cocoa. Using a metal spoon, stir until the ingredients are just combined and the mixture is almost smooth.

3 Spoon the mixture into a piping bag fitted with a fluted 1 cm (½ inch) wide piping nozzle and pipe swirls about 3 cm (1¼ inch) in diameter onto the prepared trays. Top each swirl with mixed peel. Bake for 12 minutes. Cool the cookies on the trays.

Plum and Caraway Cookies

Makes 24

80 g (2³/₄ oz) unsalted butter, softened
60 g (2¹/₄ oz/¹/₂ cup) cream cheese, chopped
115 g (4 oz/¹/₂ cup) caster (superfine) sugar
1 teaspoon natural vanilla extract
2 egg yolks
1¹/₂ teaspoons caraway seeds
150 g (5¹/₂ oz/1¹/₄ cups) plain (all-purpose) flour
plum jam, to spread
icing (confectioners') sugar, to dust

1 Cream the butter, cream cheese and sugar in a bowl using electric beaters until pale and fluffy. Add the vanilla extract and one egg yolk and beat to combine well. Add the caraway seeds and flour and stir until a dough forms. Turn the dough out onto a lightly floured work surface, form into a flat rectangle, then cover with plastic wrap and refrigerate for 2 hours, or until firm.

2 Preheat the oven to 180°C (350°F/Gas 4). Lightly grease two baking trays. Combine the remaining egg yolk with 2 teaspoons water and stir to combine well.

3 Cut the dough in half, then roll out each half on a lightly floured surface to form an 18 x 24 cm (7 x 9¹/₂ inch) rectangle. Using a sharp knife, cut the dough into 6 cm (2¹/₂ inch) squares. Place a scant teaspoon of jam diagonally across the centre of each square, then brush all four corners of the square with the egg yolk mixture. Take one corner and fold it into the centre. Take the opposite corner and fold it into the centre, overlapping the first corner, to partially enclose the jam.

4 Brush the tops of the cookies with the egg mixture, then place them, seam side up, on the baking trays. Bake for 10–12 minutes, or until light golden, swapping the position of the trays halfway through cooking. Cool on the trays for 5 minutes, then transfer to a wire rack to cool completely. Dust with icing sugar before serving.

These cookies will keep, stored in an airtight container, for up to 7 days.

Spicy Wholemeal Twists

Makes 40

125 g (4¹/₂ oz/1 cup) self-raising flour
60 g (2¹/₄ oz/¹/₂ cup) wholemeal (whole-wheat) self-raising flour
30 g (1 oz/¹/₄ cup) walnuts, ground
125 g (4¹/₂ oz) unsalted butter, cubed
60 g (2¹/₄ oz/¹/₃ cup) soft brown sugar
3 teaspoons mixed (pumpkin pie) spice
1 egg, lightly beaten
1 tablespoon sugar

1 Preheat the oven to 180°C (350°F/Gas 4). Brush two baking trays with melted butter or oil.

2 Place the flours, walnuts, butter, sugar and mixed spice in a food processor. Using the pulse action, process for 10 seconds, or until the mixture is light and crumbly. Add the egg and process for a further 10 seconds, or until just combined.

3 Transfer the mixture to a bowl, pressing together to form a soft dough. Cover with plastic wrap and refrigerate for 30 minutes, or until firm.

4 Roll 2 teaspoons of mixture into 14 cm (5¹/₂ inch) lengths. Fold the lengths in half. Twist and press the ends together. Place onto the prepared trays and sprinkle with the sugar. Bake for 15 minutes, or until golden. Transfer the cookies to a wire rack to cool.

Viennese Fingers

Makes 20

100 g (3¹/2 oz) unsalted butter, softened
40 g (1¹/2 oz/¹/3 cup) icing (confectioners') sugar
2 egg yolks
1¹/2 teaspoons natural vanilla extract
125 g (4¹/2 oz/1 cup) plain (all-purpose) flour
100 g (3¹/2 oz/²/3 cup) chopped dark cooking chocolate
30 g (1 oz) unsalted butter, extra

1   Preheat the oven to 180°C (350°F/Gas 4). Line two baking trays with baking paper. Cream the butter and icing sugar in a small bowl with electric beaters until light and fluffy. Gradually add the egg yolks and vanilla extract and beat thoroughly. Transfer to a large bowl, then sift in the flour. Using a knife, mix until the ingredients are just combined and the mixture is smooth.

2   Spoon the mixture into a piping bag fitted with a fluted 1 cm (¹/2 inch) piping nozzle and pipe the mixture into wavy 6 cm (2¹/2 inch) lengths on the trays. Bake for 12 minutes, or until golden brown. Cool slightly on the trays, then transfer to a wire rack to cool completely.

3   Place the chocolate and extra butter in a small heatproof bowl. Half-fill a saucepan with water and bring to the boil, then remove from the heat. Sit the bowl over the pan, making sure the base of the bowl does not sit in the water. Stir occasionally until the chocolate and butter have melted and the mixture is smooth. Dip half of each cookie into the melted chocolate mixture and leave to set on a sheet of baking paper or foil. Store in an airtight container for up to 2 days.

sticky toffee slice rocky road slice chocolat

Slices, bars and bakes

vnies vanilla slice chocolate peanut squares

Cherry Coconut Slice

Makes 30 pieces

125 g (4½ oz/1 cup) self-raising flour
90 g (3¼ oz/1 cup) desiccated coconut
115 g (4 oz/½ cup) caster (superfine) sugar
125 g (4½ oz) unsalted butter, melted
50 g (1¾ oz/⅓ cup) chopped dark chocolate

CHERRY TOPPING
240 g (8½ oz/1 cup) glacé (candied) cherries, finely chopped
45 g (1½ oz/¼ cup) soft brown sugar
45 g (1½ oz/½ cup) desiccated coconut
60 g (2¼ oz/½ cup) pecans, chopped
2 eggs, lightly beaten

1 Preheat the oven to 180°C (250°F/Gas 4). Brush a 30 x 25 x 2 cm (12 x 10 x ¾ inch) shallow Swiss (jelly) roll tin with melted butter or oil.

2 Combine the sifted flour, coconut and sugar in a bowl. Add the butter and stir until combined. Press the mixture into the prepared tin.

3 To make the cherry topping, combine the cherries, sugar, coconut and pecans in a bowl. Add the eggs and stir until combined. Spread evenly over the mixture in the tin.

4 Bake for 20 minutes, or until the top turns light golden. Cool in the tin. Place the chocolate in a small heatproof bowl over simmering water and stir until the chocolate is melted and smooth. Drizzle the chocolate in a criss-cross pattern over the top of the slice. Cut into 5 x 5 cm (2 x 2 inch) squares to serve.

Chocolate Caramel Slice

Makes 24 triangles

200 g (7 oz/1²/₃ cups) crushed plain chocolate biscuits (cookies)
100 g (3¹/₂ oz) unsalted butter, melted
2 tablespoons desiccated coconut
125 g (4¹/₂ oz) unsalted butter, extra
400 ml (14 fl oz) tinned sweetened condensed milk
90 g (3¹/₄ oz/¹/₃ cup) caster (superfine) sugar
3 tablespoons golden syrup or maple syrup
250 g (9 oz/1²/₃ cups) chopped dark chocolate
2 teaspoons oil

1   Grease a 30 x 20 cm (12 x 8 inch) shallow baking tin and line with baking paper, leaving it hanging over the two long sides. Combine the crushed biscuits, butter and coconut in a bowl, then press into the tin and smooth the surface.

2   Combine the extra butter, condensed milk, sugar and golden syrup in a small saucepan. Stir over low heat for 15 minutes, or until the sugar has dissolved and the mixture is smooth, thick and lightly coloured. Remove from the heat and cool slightly. Pour over the biscuit base and smooth the surface. Refrigerate for 30 minutes, or until firm.

3   Place the chocolate in a heatproof bowl. Bring a saucepan of water to the boil and remove from the heat. Sit the bowl over the saucepan, making sure the bowl doesn't touch the water. Allow to stand, stirring occasionally, until the chocolate has melted. Add the oil and stir until smooth. Spread over the caramel and leave until partially set before marking into 24 triangles. Refrigerate until firm. Cut into triangles before serving.

Sticky Toffee Slice

Makes 18 pieces

250 g (9 oz/1½ cups) pitted dates, roughly chopped
1 teaspoon bicarbonate of soda (baking soda)
215 g (7½ oz) unsalted butter
185 g (6½ oz/1½ cups) self-raising flour
1 teaspoon natural vanilla extract
1 teaspoon baking powder
3 eggs
90 ml (3 fl oz) milk
2 tablespoons soft brown sugar
90 g (3¼ oz/¾ cup) icing (confectioners') sugar
90 g (3¼ oz/¾ cup) walnuts, chopped

1   Preheat the oven to 180°C (350°F/Gas 4). Lightly grease a 20 x 30 cm (8 x 12 inch) baking tin and line with baking paper, leaving it hanging over the two long sides. Place the dates in a saucepan with 200 ml (7 fl oz) water, bring to the boil, reduce the heat and simmer for 10 minutes—make sure the water doesn't evaporate completely. Add the bicarbonate of soda and leave to cool.

2   Place 185 g (6½ oz) of the butter, flour, vanilla extract, baking powder, eggs and 80 ml (2½ fl oz/⅓ cup) of the milk in a food processor and mix for 1 minute. Add the dates and pulse to blend. Place the mixture in the tin and bake for 20 minutes, or until a skewer inserted in the centre comes out clean. Set aside to cool.

3   Place the remaining butter, milk and brown sugar in a saucepan and heat to dissolve the sugar. Add the icing sugar and mix well. Spread over the cooled slice and sprinkle with the walnuts.

Chewy Fruit and Seed Slice

Makes 18 pieces

200 g (7 oz) unsalted butter

175 g (6 oz/1/2 cup) golden syrup or maple syrup

125 g (41/2 oz/1/2 cup) crunchy peanut butter

2 teaspoons natural vanilla extract

30 g (1 oz/1/4 cup) plain (all-purpose) flour

30 g (1 oz/1/3 cup) ground almonds

1/2 teaspoon mixed (pumpkin pie) spice

300 g (101/2 oz/3 cups) rolled (porridge) oats

2 teaspoons finely grated orange zest

185 g (61/2 oz/1 cup) soft brown sugar

45 g (11/2 oz/1/2 cup) desiccated coconut

50 g (13/4 oz/1/3 cup) sesame seeds, toasted

90 g (31/4 oz/2/3 cup) pepitas (pumpkin seeds) or shelled sunflower seeds

80 g (23/4 oz/2/3 cup) raisins, chopped

45 g (11/2 oz/1/4 cup) mixed peel

1   Preheat the oven to 170°C (325°F/Gas 3). Lightly grease a 20 x 30 cm (8 x 12 inch) shallow tin and line with baking paper, leaving it hanging over the two long sides.

2   Place the butter and golden syrup in a small saucepan over low heat, stirring occasionally until melted. Remove from the heat and stir in the peanut butter and vanilla extract until combined.

3   Mix together the remaining ingredients, stirring well. Make a well in the centre and add the butter and syrup mixture. Mix with a large metal spoon until combined. Press evenly into the tin and bake for 25 minutes, or until golden. Cool in the tin, then cut into squares.

Rocky Road Slice

Makes 24 pieces

150 g (5^1/$_2$ oz) unsalted butter, cubed and softened
125 g (4^1/$_2$ oz/heaped ^{1}/$_2$ cup) sugar
1 egg, lightly beaten
50 g (1^3/$_4$ oz/^{1}/$_3$ cup) chopped dark chocolate, melted
125 g (4^1/$_2$ oz/1 cup) self-raising flour
2 tablespoons unsweetened cocoa powder
250 g (9 oz/1^2/$_3$ cups) chopped dark chocolate, extra
25 g (1 oz) unsalted butter, extra
105 g (3^1/$_2$ oz/^{1}/$_2$ cup) glacé (candied) cherries, cut in half
50 g (1^3/$_4$ oz/1 cup) mini marshmallows
80 g (2^3/$_4$ oz/^{1}/$_2$ cup) unsalted peanuts

1   Preheat the oven to 180°C (350°F/Gas 4). Lightly grease two
    26 x 8 x 4.5 cm (10^1/$_2$ x 3^1/$_4$ x 1^3/$_4$ inch) loaf (bar) tins and line with
    baking paper, leaving the paper hanging over the two long sides.

2   Cream the butter and sugar in a small bowl with electric beaters until
    light and fluffy. Beat in the egg and melted chocolate and transfer to
    a large bowl. Using a metal spoon, fold in the combined sifted flour
    and cocoa and mix well. Divide the mixture between the prepared
    tins, smoothing the surface. Bake for 20–25 minutes. Gently press
    down the outer edges of the slice, using the back of a spoon, to make
    the surface level. Leave to cool in the tins for 30 minutes.

3   Place the extra chocolate and butter in a heatproof bowl. Half-fill a
    saucepan with water, bring to the boil, then remove from the heat.
    Sit the bowl over the saucepan, making sure the base of the bowl
    does not sit in the water. Stir occasionally until the mixture has

melted and is smooth. Spread the mixture over the slice bases, using about a third of the chocolate altogether. Top each randomly with cherries, marshmallows and peanuts, then spoon the remaining chocolate evenly over the tops. Tap the tins on a bench to distribute the chocolate evenly. Leave to set, lift out using the paper as handles, then cut into 2 cm (3/4 inch) wide fingers for serving.

 Rocky road slice will keep in an airtight container in a cool, dark place for up to 4 days.

Chocolate Brownies

Makes 24 pieces

40 g (1$^{1}/_{2}$ oz/$^{1}/_{3}$ cup) plain (all-purpose) flour

60 g (2$^{1}/_{4}$ oz/$^{1}/_{2}$ cup) unsweetened cocoa powder

500 g (1 lb 2 oz/2$^{1}/_{4}$ cups) sugar

125 g (4$^{1}/_{2}$ oz/1 cup) chopped pecans or walnuts

250 g (9 oz/1$^{2}/_{3}$ cups) finely chopped dark chocolate

250 g (9 oz) unsalted butter, melted

2 teaspoons natural vanilla extract

4 eggs, lightly beaten

1 Preheat the oven to 180°C (350°F/Gas 4). Lightly grease a 20 x 30 cm (8 x 12 inch) baking tin and line with baking paper, leaving the paper hanging over the two long sides.

2 Sift the flour and cocoa into a bowl and add the sugar, nuts and chocolate. Mix together and make a well in the centre. Pour the butter onto the dry ingredients with the vanilla extract and eggs and mix well.

3 Spoon the mixture into the prepared tin, smooth the surface and bake for 50 minutes (it will still be a bit soft on the inside). Chill for at least 2 hours before lifting out, using the paper as handles, and cutting into pieces.

Chocolate Hedgehog Slice

Makes 24 pieces

250 g (9 oz/2 cups) finely crushed chocolate cream biscuits (cookies)
45 g (1¹/2 oz/¹/2 cup) desiccated coconut
125 g (4¹/2 oz/1 cup) pecans, roughly chopped
1 tablespoon unsweetened cocoa powder, sifted
100 g (3¹/2 oz/²/3 cup) chopped dark chocolate
80 g (2³/4 oz) unsalted butter
1 tablespoon golden syrup or maple syrup
1 egg, lightly beaten
50 g (1³/4 oz/¹/3 cup) dark chocolate melts (buttons)
butter, extra
extra pecans, to decorate

1   Line the base and sides of a 30 x 20 cm (12 x 8 inch) baking tin with foil. Combine the biscuit crumbs, coconut, pecans and cocoa in a bowl. Make a well in the centre.

2   Combine the chocolate, butter and syrup in a small heavy-based saucepan. Stir over low heat until the chocolate and butter have melted and the mixture is smooth. Pour the mixture and egg into the dry ingredients. Stir until well combined. Press the mixture evenly into the prepared tin. Refrigerate for 30 minutes, or until set.

3   To make the icing, place the chocolate melts and butter in a small heatproof bowl. Stand over a saucepan of simmering water. Stir until melted and smooth. Cool slightly. Spread mixture evenly over the slice and refrigerate until set. Remove the slice from the tin and cut into small squares with a sharp knife. Decorate with pecans dipped in extra melted chocolate.

Passionfruit and Coconut Cheese Slice

Makes 24 pieces

100 g (3^1/$_2$ oz/^{3}/$_4$ cup) slivered almonds
125 g (4^1/$_2$ oz/1 cup) plain (all-purpose) flour
1 teaspoon baking powder
100 g (3^1/$_2$ oz) unsalted butter, chopped
125 g (4^1/$_2$ oz/^{1}/$_2$ cup) caster (superfine) sugar
1 egg yolk
25 g (1 oz/^{1}/$_4$ cup) desiccated coconut
750 g (1 lb 10 oz/3 cups) cream cheese, softened
2 eggs, extra
185 ml (6 fl oz/^{3}/$_4$ cup) coconut milk
3 teaspoons natural vanilla extract
^{1}/$_2$ teaspoon lemon juice
185 g (6^1/$_2$ oz/^{3}/$_4$ cup) caster (superfine) sugar, extra
65 g (2^1/$_4$ oz/^{3}/$_4$ cup) flaked almonds, toasted

TOPPING
90 g (3^1/$_4$ oz/^{3}/$_4$ cup) icing (confectioners') sugar
40 g (1^1/$_2$ oz) unsalted butter, softened
1 tablespoon cornflour (cornstarch)
2 tablespoons strained passionfruit juice

1 Finely chop the almonds in a food processor. Sift the flour and baking powder into a bowl. Rub the butter into the flour until it resembles breadcrumbs. Stir in the chopped almonds and sugar. Make a well in the centre and add the egg yolk. Mix with a flat-bladed knife until the mixture comes together in beads. Remove to a lightly floured work surface and shape into a ball. Flatten slightly, cover with plastic wrap and refrigerate for 30 minutes.

2 Preheat the oven to 170°C (325°F/Gas 3). Grease a 30 x 20 x 5 cm (12 x 8 x 2 inch) baking tin and line with baking paper, leaving it hanging over the two long sides. Roll the dough out to fit the tin and press in evenly. Sprinkle the coconut over and lightly press it in. Bake for 10 minutes, then cool for 10 minutes.

3 Combine the cream cheese and extra eggs in a food processor. Add the coconut milk, vanilla extract, lemon juice and the extra sugar, and blend until smooth. Pour over the base. Bake for 40 minutes. Cool in the tin.

4 To make the topping, mix the icing sugar and butter with a wooden spoon until smooth. Stir in the cornflour, then the passionfruit juice. Mix until smooth, then spread over the slice. Scatter the toasted almonds over. Leave to set, then cut into 5 cm (2 inch) squares.

Vanilla Slice

Makes 9 pieces

500 g (1 lb 2 oz) ready-made puff pastry

250 g (9 oz/1 heaped cup) caster (superfine) sugar

90 g (3¼ oz/¾ cup) cornflour (cornstarch)

60 g (2¼ oz/½ cup) custard powder (instant vanilla pudding mix)

1 litre (35 fl oz/4 cups) pouring (whipping) cream

60 g (2¼ oz) unsalted butter, cubed

2 teaspoons natural vanilla extract

3 egg yolks

ICING

185 g (6½ oz/1½ cups) icing (confectioners') sugar

60 g (2¼ oz/¼ cup) passionfruit pulp

15 g (½ oz) unsalted butter, melted

1 Preheat the oven to 210°C (415°F/Gas 6–7). Grease two baking trays with oil. Line the base and side of a shallow 23 cm (9 inch) square cake tin with foil, leaving the foil hanging over on two opposite sides.

2 Divide the pastry in half, roll each piece to a 25 cm (10 inch) square about 3 mm (⅛ inch) thick and place each one on a prepared tray. Prick all over with a fork and bake for 8 minutes, or until golden. Trim each pastry sheet to a 23 cm (9 inch) square. Place one sheet, top side down, in the cake tin.

3 Combine the sugar, cornflour and custard powder in a saucepan. Gradually add the cream and stir until smooth. Place over medium heat and stir constantly for 2 minutes, or until the mixture boils and thickens. Add the butter and vanilla extract and stir until smooth.

Remove from the heat and whisk in the egg yolks until combined. Spread the custard over the pastry in the tin and cover with the remaining pastry, top side down. Allow to cool.

4   To make the icing, combine the icing sugar, passionfruit pulp and butter in a small bowl and stir together until smooth. Lift the slice out, using the foil as handles. Spread the icing over the top and leave it to set before carefully cutting into squares with a serrated knife.

Chocolate Peanut Squares

Makes 24 squares

200 g (7 oz/1¹/₃ cups) chopped dark chocolate
125 g (4¹/₂ oz) unsalted butter
230 g (8¹/₄ oz/1 cup firmly packed) soft brown sugar
65 g (2¹/₄ oz/¹/₄ cup) crunchy peanut butter
2 eggs
125 g (4¹/₂ oz/1 cup) plain (all-purpose) flour
30 g (1 oz/¹/₄ cup) self-raising flour
80 g (2³/₄ oz/¹/₂ cup) unsalted roasted peanuts, roughly chopped
100 g (3¹/₂ oz/²/₃ cup) chopped dark chocolate, extra

1 Preheat the oven to 170°C (325°F/Gas 3). Lightly grease an 18 x 27 cm (7 x 10³/₄ inch) baking tin and line with baking paper, leaving it hanging over the two long sides.

2 Place the chocolate in a heatproof bowl. Bring a saucepan of water to the boil and remove from the heat. Sit the bowl over the pan— ensure the bowl doesn't touch the water. Allow to stand, stirring occasionally until melted. Allow to cool.

3 Cream the butter, sugar and peanut butter with electric beaters until thick. Add the eggs one at a time, beating well after each addition. Stir in the melted chocolate, sifted flours and peanuts.

4 Spread the mixture into the prepared tin and gently press the chocolate evenly into the surface. Bake for 30 minutes, or until a skewer inserted into the centre comes out clean. Cool in the tin.

Apple Crumble Slice

Makes 15 pieces

90 g (3¼ oz/¾ cup) self-raising flour
90 g (3¼ oz/¾ cup) plain (all-purpose) flour
90 g (3¼ oz/1 cup) desiccated coconut
150 g (5½ oz) unsalted butter
140 g (5 oz/¾ cup) soft brown sugar
410 g (14½ oz) tinned pie apple
35 g (1¼ oz/⅓ cup) rolled (porridge) oats
35 g (1¼ oz/¼ cup) currants
¼ teaspoon ground cinnamon

1 Preheat the oven to 180°C (350°F/Gas 4). Brush an 18 x 27 cm (7 x 10¾ inch) baking tin with melted butter or oil. Line the base and sides with baking paper, leaving it hanging over two sides.

2 Sift the flours into a large bowl and add the coconut. Combine the butter and sugar in a small saucepan. Stir over low heat until the butter has melted and the sugar has dissolved; remove from the heat. Pour the butter mixture into the coconut mixture. Using a wooden spoon, stir until well combined.

3 Reserve 1 cup of the coconut mixture. Press the remaining mixture into the prepared tin, smoothing the surface with the back of a spoon. Bake for 10 minutes, then allow to cool completely.

4 Spread the pie apple over the cooled base. Combine the reserved mixture with the oats and currants. Using your fingertips, crumble the mixture and sprinkle over the apple. Dust with cinnamon. Bake for 30 minutes, or until the top is golden. Cool, lift from the tin and cut into squares.

Princess Fingers

Makes 24 pieces

125 g (4½ oz) unsalted butter, cubed and softened
90 g (3¼ oz/⅓ cup) caster (superfine) sugar
1 teaspoon natural vanilla extract
2 egg yolks
250 g (9 oz/2 cups) plain (all-purpose) flour
1 teaspoon baking powder
1 tablespoon milk
160 g (5¾ oz/½ cup) raspberry jam
40 g (1½ oz/⅓ cup) walnuts, chopped
80 g (2¾ oz/⅓ cup) red glacé (candied) cherries, chopped

COCONUT MERINGUE
2 egg whites
125 g (4½ oz/½ cup) caster (superfine) sugar
1 tablespoon grated orange zest
45 g (1½ oz/½ cup) desiccated coconut
30 g (1 oz/1 cup) puffed rice cereal

1   Preheat the oven to 180°C (350°F/Gas 4). Lightly grease a
    20 x 30 cm (8 x 12 inch) shallow baking tin and line with baking
    paper, leaving it hanging over the two long sides.

2   Cream the butter, sugar and vanilla extract with electric beaters until
    light and fluffy. Add the egg yolks one at a time, beating well after
    each addition. Sift the flour and baking powder into a bowl, then fold
    into the butter mixture with a metal spoon. Fold in the milk, then
    press evenly and firmly into the prepared tin. Spread the jam over the
    surface and sprinkle with the chopped walnuts and cherries.

3 To make the coconut meringue, beat the egg whites in a small, dry bowl until stiff peaks form. Fold in the sugar and orange zest with a metal spoon, then fold in the coconut and puffed rice cereal. Spread over the slice with a metal spatula.

4 Bake for 30–35 minutes, or until firm and golden brown. Cool the slice in the tin before lifting out, using the paper as handles, and cutting into fingers.

This slice will keep for up to 4 days in an airtight container.

Coconut Jam Slice

Makes 25 pieces

185 g (6¹/₂ oz/1¹/₂ cups) plain (all-purpose) flour
150 g (5¹/₂ oz) unsalted butter
60 g (2¹/₄ oz/¹/₂ cup) icing (confectioners') sugar

TOPPING
80 g (2³/₄ oz/¹/₃ cup) caster (superfine) sugar
2 eggs
180 g (6 oz/2 cups) desiccated coconut
105 g (3¹/₂ oz/¹/₃ cup) blackberry jam

1 Preheat the oven to 180°C (350°F/Gas 4). Brush a 23 cm (9 inch) square cake tin with melted butter or oil. Line the base and side with baking paper, leaving it hanging over two sides.

2 Place the flour, butter and icing sugar in a food processor. Using the pulse action, process for 30 seconds, or until the mixture forms a dough. Turn out onto a lightly floured surface and knead for 20 seconds, or until smooth. Press into the prepared tin and refrigerate for 10 minutes. Bake for 15 minutes, or until just golden, and then cool.

3 To make the topping, place the sugar and eggs in a bowl and whisk until combined. Stir in the coconut.

4 Spread the jam over the cooled base. Spread the topping over the jam, pressing down with the back of a spoon. Bake for 20 minutes, or until light golden. Cut into 25 squares when cool.

Date and Cinnamon Cubes

Makes 36 pieces

600 g (1 lb 5 oz/3³/4 cups) chopped pitted dates
1 teaspoon bicarbonate of soda (baking soda)
125 g (4¹/2 oz) unsalted butter, chopped
155 g (5¹/2 oz/³/4 cup) soft brown sugar
2 eggs
125 g (4¹/2 oz/1 cup) plain (all-purpose) flour
60 g (2¹/4 oz/¹/2 cup) self-raising flour
¹/2 teaspoon ground cinnamon, plus ¹/2 teaspoon, extra
60 g (2¹/4 oz/¹/2 cup) icing (confectioners') sugar

1 Preheat the oven to 180°C (350°F/Gas 4). Lightly grease a 23 cm (9 inch) square shallow tin and line the base with baking paper.

2 Combine the dates and 500 ml (17 fl oz/2 cups) water in a saucepan, bring to the boil, then remove from the heat. Stir in the bicarbonate of soda and mix well. Cool to room temperature.

3 Cream the butter and sugar in a large bowl using electric beaters until pale and fluffy. Add the eggs one at a time, beating well after each addition. Sift the flours and cinnamon into a bowl, then fold into the butter mixture alternately with the date mixture. Spread into the prepared tin. Bake for 55–60 minutes, or until a skewer inserted into the centre comes out clean. Cool in the tin for 5 minutes, then turn out onto a wire rack to cool completely.

4 Cut into 36 pieces and place on a sheet of baking paper. Sift the combined icing sugar and extra cinnamon over the cubes and toss to coat. Serve immediately (the coating will be absorbed into the cakes quite quickly if left to stand).

Fruit and Nut Slice

125 g (4 1/2 oz / 1 cup) plain (all-purpose) flour
60 g (2 1/4 oz) unsalted butter, cubed
80 g (2 3/4 oz / 1/3 cup) caster (superfine) sugar
1 teaspoon grated lemon zest
2 tablespoons sour cream

FRUIT AND NUT TOPPING
160 g (5 3/4 oz / 1 cup) raisins, finely chopped
40 g (1 1/2 oz / 1/4 cup) pitted dates, finely chopped
40 g (1 1/2 oz / 1/4 cup) dried figs, finely chopped
85 g (3 oz / 2/3 cup) walnuts, chopped
25 g (1 oz / 1/4 cup) flaked almonds
2 tablespoons lemon juice
1 egg
60 g (2 1/4 oz / 1/3 cup) soft brown sugar
2 tablespoons plain (all-purpose) flour

1   Preheat the oven to 180°C (350°F/Gas 4). Brush a shallow 30 x 20 cm
    (12 x 8 inch) cake tin with melted butter or oil. Cover the base with
    baking paper, leaving it hanging over two sides, and then grease
    the paper.

2   Sift the flour into a mixing bowl and add the butter, sugar and lemon
    zest. Using your fingertips, rub the butter into the flour for 3 minutes,
    or until the mixture is fine and crumbly. Add the cream and press
    together to form a soft dough.

3 Press the mixture into the prepared tin and smooth the surface, pricking evenly with a fork. Bake for 15 minutes, or until just golden.

4 To make the fruit and nut topping, combine the fruits and nuts with the lemon juice in a large bowl. Using electric beaters, beat the egg and sugar in a small bowl for 15 minutes, or until thick and foamy. Transfer the egg mixture into the bowl with fruit and add the sifted flour. Stir with a wooden spoon until just combined. Spread over the topping. Return to the oven and bake for a further 30 minutes. Remove from the oven and cool in the tin. Cut into 18 diagonal fingers before serving.

 You can use a combination of different nuts in place of walnuts. Store the slice in an airtight container for up to 2 days.

Ginger and Pistachio Squares

Makes 15 squares

125 g (4¹/2 oz) unsalted butter
185 g (6¹/2 oz/1 cup) soft brown sugar
2 eggs, lightly beaten
155 g (5¹/2 oz/1¹/4 cups) self-raising flour
1¹/2 tablespoons ground ginger

WHITE CHOCOLATE ICING
150 g (5¹/2 oz/1 cup) chopped white chocolate
60 ml (2 fl oz/¹/4 cup) pouring (whipping) cream
2 tablespoons chopped glacé (candied) ginger
2 tablespoons chopped pistachios

1 Preheat the oven to 180°C (350°F/Gas4). Brush a shallow 27 x 18 cm (10³/4 x 7 inch) cake tin with melted butter or oil. Cover the base with baking paper, leaving it hanging over two sides, then grease the paper.

2 Using electric beaters, cream the butter and sugar in a small mixing bowl until light and fluffy. Add the egg gradually, beating thoroughly after each addition. Transfer the mixture to a large bowl. Using a metal spoon, fold in the sifted flour and ginger and stir until just combined.

3 Spread the mixture into the prepared tin. Bake for 30 minutes, or until golden and firm in the centre. Allow to cool in the tin.

4 To make the icing, combine the chocolate and cream in a small pan. Stir over low heat until chocolate has melted and mixture is smooth. Cool. Using a flat-bladed knife, spread evenly over slice. Sprinkle with ginger and pistachios; allow icing to set, then cut into squares.

Fruit Mince Slice

Makes 15 pieces

250 g (9 oz/2 cups) plain (all-purpose) flour
60 g (2¼ oz/½ cup) icing (confectioners') sugar
185 g (6½ oz) unsalted butter, cubed
1 egg
410 g (14½ oz) tinned fruit mince
150 g (5½ oz/⅔ cup) pitted prunes, chopped
100 g (3½ oz/½ cup) glacé ginger, chopped
1 egg, lightly beaten, extra
icing (confectioners') sugar, to dust

1 Preheat the oven to 190°C (375°F/Gas 5). Lightly grease a shallow 28 x 18 cm (11¼ x 7 inch) baking tin and line the base with baking paper, leaving it hanging over the two long sides.

2 Sift the flour and icing sugar into a large bowl. Rub in the butter with your fingertips until the mixture resembles fine breadcrumbs. Make a well in the centre and add the egg. Mix with a flat-bladed knife, using a cutting action, until the mixture comes together. Turn out onto a lightly floured surface and press together until smooth.

3 Divide the dough in half and press one portion into the tin. Bake for 10 minutes, then leave to cool. Roll the remaining pastry out on a piece of baking paper and refrigerate for 15 minutes. Spread the fruit mince evenly over the baked pastry, topping with the prunes and ginger.

4 Cut the rolled pastry into thin strips with a sharp knife or fluted pastry wheel. Arrange on top of the fruit in a diagonal lattice pattern. Brush with beaten egg. Bake for 30 minutes, or until golden. Cool in the tin and cut into squares or fingers. Serve dusted with icing sugar.

Lemon Squares

Makes 30 squares

125 g (4¹/2 oz) unsalted butter
75 g (2¹/2 oz / ¹/3 cup) caster (superfine) sugar
155 g (5¹/2 oz / 1¹/4 cups) plain (all-purpose) flour, sifted
icing (confectioners') sugar, to dust

TOPPING
4 eggs, lightly beaten
250 g (9 oz / 1 heaped cup) caster (superfine) sugar
60 ml (2 fl oz / ¹/4 cup) lemon juice
1 teaspoon finely grated lemon zest
30 g (1 oz / ¹/4 cup) plain (all-purpose) flour
¹/2 teaspoon baking powder

1   Preheat the oven to 180°C (350°F/Gas 4). Lightly grease a 20 x 30 cm
    (8 x 12 inch) baking tin and line with baking paper, leaving it hanging
    over two opposite sides.

2   Cream the butter and sugar with electric beaters until pale and fluffy.
    Fold in the flour with a metal spoon. Press into the prepared tin and
    bake for 20 minutes, or until golden and firm. Leave to cool.

3   To make the topping, cream the eggs and sugar with electric beaters
    for 2 minutes, or until light and fluffy. Stir in the lemon juice and
    lemon zest. Sift together the flour and baking powder and gradually
    whisk into the egg mixture. Pour onto the pastry base. Bake for
    25 minutes, or until just firm. Cool in the tin and dust with
    icing sugar.

Fig and Cinnamon Slice

Makes 15 pieces

125 g (4¹/₂ oz) unsalted butter, softened
55 g (2 oz/¹/₄ cup firmly packed) soft brown sugar
1 teaspoon ground cinnamon
185 g (6¹/₂ oz/1¹/₂ cups) plain (all-purpose) flour
375 g (13 oz/2¹/₃ cups) dried figs
1 cinnamon stick
125 g (4¹/₂ oz/¹/₂ cup) caster (superfine) sugar
375 ml (13 fl oz/1¹/₂ cups) boiling water

1   Preheat the oven to 180°C (350°F/Gas 4). Lightly grease an 18 x 27 cm (7 x 10³/₄ inch) baking tin and line with baking paper, leaving it hanging over the two long sides.

2   Cream the butter, sugar and ground cinnamon until light and fluffy, then fold in the flour with a large metal spoon. Press the mixture evenly into the prepared tin and bake for 25 minutes. Cool slightly.

3   Place the figs, cinnamon stick, sugar and boiling water in a saucepan, mix together and bring to the boil. Reduce the heat and simmer for 20 minutes, or until the figs have softened and the water has reduced by one-third. Remove the cinnamon stick and place the mixture in a food processor. Process in short bursts until smooth.

4   Pour the fig mixture onto the pastry base and bake for 10 minutes, or until set. Cool in the tin, then lift out and cut into squares.

Coffee Pecan Slice

Makes 15 pieces

185 g (6¹/2 oz/1¹/2 cups) plain (all-purpose) flour
60 g (2¹/4 oz/¹/2 cup) icing (confectioners') sugar
150 g (5¹/2 oz) unsalted butter

TOPPING
2 tablespoons golden syrup or dark corn syrup
2 tablespoons pouring (whipping) cream
60 g (2¹/4 oz/¹/3 cup) soft brown sugar
75 g (2¹/2 oz) unsalted butter, melted
2 eggs, lightly beaten
1 teaspoon instant coffee powder
200 g (7 oz/2 cups) pecans

1   Preheat the oven to 180°C (350°F/Gas 4). Brush an 18 x 27 cm
    (7 x 10³/4 inch) shallow baking tin with melted butter or oil.
    Line with baking paper, leaving it hanging over two sides.

2   Place the flour, icing sugar and butter in a food processor.
    Using the pulse action, process for 1 minute, or until the mixture
    comes together. Turn out onto a lightly floured surface and knead
    gently for 30 seconds, or until smooth. Press the mixture
    into the prepared tin and bake for 15 minutes, or until just golden.
    Cool completely in the tin on a wire rack.

3   To make the topping, combine the golden syrup, cream, sugar, butter,
    eggs and coffee in a bowl and beat with a wooden spoon until
    smooth. Add the pecans and stir to combine. Pour onto the pastry
    base and bake for a further 25 minutes, or until set. Cool completely in
    the tin. Lift out and cut into squares, using a sharp knife.

Macadamia Blondies

Makes 25 pieces

100 g (3¹/2 oz) unsalted butter, cubed
100 g (3¹/2 oz/²/3 cup) chopped white chocolate
125 g (4¹/2 oz/¹/2 cup) caster (superfine) sugar
2 eggs, lightly beaten
1 teaspoon natural vanilla extract
125 g (4¹/2 oz/1 cup) self-raising flour
80 g (2³/4 oz/¹/2 cup) macadamia nuts, roughly chopped

1 Preheat the oven to 180°C (350°F/Gas 4). Lightly grease a 20 cm (8 inch) square tin and line with baking paper, leaving it hanging over two opposite sides.

2 Place the butter and chocolate in a heatproof bowl. Half-fill a saucepan with water and bring to the boil. Remove from the heat. Place the bowl over the saucepan, making sure the base of the bowl does not sit in the water. Stir occasionally until the butter and chocolate have melted and are smooth.

3 Add the sugar and gradually stir in the eggs. Add the vanilla extract, fold in the flour and macadamia nuts, then pour into the prepared tin. Bake for 35–40 minutes. If the top starts to brown too quickly, cover lightly with a sheet of foil. When cooked, cool in the tin before lifting out, using the paper as handles, and cutting into squares.

Extra melted white chocolate can be drizzled over the top, if desired.

Caramel Date Shortcake

Makes 12 pieces

125 g (4¹/2 oz) unsalted butter, softened
125 g (4¹/2 oz/¹/2 cup) caster (superfine) sugar
1 teaspoon natural vanilla extract
1 egg
250 g (9 oz/2 cups) plain (all-purpose) flour
1 teaspoon baking powder
175 g (6 oz/1 cup) roughly chopped pitted dates
1 tablespoon soft brown sugar
2 teaspoons unsweetened cocoa powder
10 g (¹/4 oz) unsalted butter, extra

1   Preheat the oven to 180°C (350°F/Gas 4). Lightly grease an 18 x 27 cm
    (7 x 10³/4 inch) shallow baking tin. Line with baking paper, leaving it
    hanging over the two long sides. Cream the butter, sugar and vanilla
    extract with electric beaters until light and fluffy. Beat in the egg,
    then transfer to a bowl. Fold in the combined sifted flour and baking
    powder in batches. Press half the dough into the prepared tin. Form
    the other half into a ball, cover and refrigerate for 30 minutes.

2   Place the dates, brown sugar, cocoa, extra butter and 250 ml (9 fl oz/
    1 cup) water in a saucepan. Bring to the boil, stirring, then reduce the
    heat and simmer, stirring, for 12 minutes, or until the dates are soft and
    the water absorbed. Spread onto a plate and refrigerate to cool quickly.

3   Spread the filling over the pastry base and grate the remaining dough
    over the top. Bake for 35 minutes, or until light brown and crisp. Cool
    in the tin for 15 minutes, then lift onto a wire rack. Cut into squares
    to serve.

Chocolate Cream Cheese Slice

Makes 18 pieces

185 g (6$^1/_2$ oz/1$^1/_2$ cups) plain (all-purpose) flour
30 g (1 oz/$^1/_4$ cup) unsweetened cocoa powder
60 g (2$^1/_4$ oz/$^1/_2$ cup) icing (confectioners') sugar
160 g (5$^3/_4$ oz) unsalted butter, cubed
1 teaspoon unsweetened cocoa powder, extra, to dust
1 teaspoon icing (confectioners') sugar, extra, to dust

FILLING
250 g (9 oz/1 cup) cream cheese
90 g (3$^1/_4$ oz/$^1/_3$ cup) sour cream
3 eggs
80 g (2$^3/_4$ oz/$^1/_3$ cup) caster (superfine) sugar
100 g (3$^1/_2$ oz/$^2/_3$ cup) grated white chocolate

1 Preheat the oven to 180°C (350°F/Gas 4). Brush a 23 cm (9 inch) shallow square cake tin with melted butter or oil. Line the base and sides with baking paper, leaving it hanging over two sides.

2 Sift the flour, cocoa and icing sugar into a bowl and add the butter. Using your fingertips, rub the butter into the flour for 5 minutes, or until the mixture forms a dough. Press into the prepared tin, smoothing the surface with the back of a metal spoon. Bake for 15 minutes, then allow to cool completely.

3 To make the filling, place all the ingredients in a food processor. Using the pulse action, process for 20 seconds, or until smooth. Pour over the base. Bake for 35 minutes, or until the filling is set. Allow to cool completely in the tin, then cut into bars. Sift the combined cocoa powder and icing sugar onto the bars to serve.

Orange, Pistachio and Semolina Slice

Makes 18 pieces

100 g (3½ oz/⅔ cup) shelled pistachios
200 g (7 oz) unsalted butter, cubed
160 g (5¾ oz/¾ cup) caster (superfine) sugar
1 teaspoon natural vanilla extract
1 tablespoon finely grated orange zest
2 eggs
60 g (2¼ oz/½ cup) self-raising flour, sifted
125 ml (4 fl oz/½ cup) orange juice
185 g (6½ oz/1½ cups) fine semolina
250 g (9 oz/1 heaped cup) caster (superfine) sugar, extra
125 ml (4 fl oz/½ cup) orange juice, extra
icing (confectioners') sugar, to dust

1 Preheat the oven to 180°C (350°F/Gas 4). Lightly grease a 20 x 30 cm (8 x 12 inch) shallow baking tin and line with baking paper, leaving it hanging over the two long sides.

2 Spread the pistachios on a baking tray and bake for 8–10 minutes, or until they are lightly toasted. Cool, then chop.

3 Cream the butter and sugar with electric beaters until light and fluffy. Add the vanilla extract, orange zest and eggs, and beat until combined. Add the flour, orange juice, semolina and pistachios, and fold in with a spatula—do not overmix. Spread into the tin. Bake for 30 minutes, or until golden brown. Cool for 10 minutes in the tin, then on a wire rack.

4 Mix the extra sugar and orange juice in a small saucepan. Bring to the boil over medium heat, then simmer for 1 minute. Spoon over the slice. Cool and cut into squares or diamonds. Dust with icing sugar.

Berry and Almond Slice

Makes 15 pieces

1 sheet ready-made puff pastry
150 g (5^1/$_2$ oz) unsalted butter
185 g (6^1/$_2$ oz/^{3}/$_4$ cup) caster (superfine) sugar
3 eggs, lightly beaten
2 tablespoons grated lemon zest
125 g (4^1/$_2$ oz/1^1/$_4$ cups) ground almonds
2 tablespoons plain (all-purpose) flour
150 g (5^1/$_2$ oz/^{2}/$_3$ cup) raspberries
150 g (5^1/$_2$ oz/^{2}/$_3$ cup) blackberries
icing (confectioners') sugar, to dust

1 Preheat the oven to 200°C (400°F/Gas 6). Lightly grease a 23 cm (9 inch) square shallow tin and line with baking paper, leaving it hanging over two opposite sides.

2 Place the pastry on a baking tray lined with baking paper. Prick the pastry all over with a fork and bake for 15 minutes, or until golden. Ease into the prepared tin, trimming the edges if necessary. Reduce the oven temperature to 180°C (350°F/Gas 4).

3 Cream the butter and sugar in a small bowl with electric beaters until light and fluffy. Gradually add the egg, beating after every addition, then the lemon zest. Fold in the almonds and flour, then spread the mixture over the pastry.

4 Scatter the fruit on top and bake for 1 hour, or until lightly golden. Cool in the tin, then lift out, using the paper as handles. Cut into pieces and dust with icing sugar.

Apricot and Macaroon Slice

Makes 16 pieces

100 g (3¹/₂ oz) unsalted butter, softened
90 g (3¹/₄ oz/¹/₃ cup) caster (superfine) sugar
1 egg
185 g (6¹/₂ oz/1¹/₂ cups) plain (all-purpose) flour
¹/₂ teaspoon baking powder

FILLING
250 g (9 oz/1¹/₃ cups) dried apricots, roughly chopped
1 tablespoon Grand Marnier
2 tablespoons caster (superfine) sugar
125 ml (4¹/₂ oz/¹/₂ cup) boiling water

TOPPING
100 g (3¹/₂ oz) unsalted butter
90 g (3¹/₄ oz/¹/₃ cup) caster (superfine) sugar
1 teaspoon natural vanilla extract
2 eggs
270 g (9¹/₂ oz/3 cups) desiccated coconut
40 g (1¹/₂ oz/¹/₃ cup) plain (all-purpose) flour
¹/₂ teaspoon baking powder

1 Preheat the oven to 180°C (350°F/Gas 4). Lightly grease a
   20 x 30 cm (8 x 12 inch) baking tin and line with baking paper.

2 Cream the butter and sugar until light and fluffy. Add the egg and
   beat well. Sift the flour and baking powder and fold into the butter
   mixture with a metal spoon. Press firmly into the prepared tin and
   bake for 20–25 minutes, or until golden brown. Cool.

3 To make the filling, combine the apricots, Grand Marnier, sugar and boiling water in a bowl. Set aside for 30 minutes, then purée in a food processor. Spread evenly over the cooled pastry base.

4 To make the topping, cream the butter, sugar and vanilla extract until light and fluffy. Gradually add the egg, beating well after each addition. Fold in the coconut, flour and baking powder with a large metal spoon. Spoon onto the apricot filling; leave the topping lumpy and loose—do not press down. Bake for 20–25 minutes, or until lightly golden.

Pecan Brownies

Makes 16 pieces

125 g (4¹/₂ oz/³/₄ cup) chopped dark chocolate
90 g (3¹/₄ oz) unsalted butter, softened
250 g (9 oz/1 heaped cup) caster (superfine) sugar
1 teaspoon natural vanilla extract
2 eggs
80 g (2³/₄ oz/²/₃ cup) plain (all-purpose) flour
30 g (1 oz/¹/₄ cup) unsweetened cocoa powder
¹/₂ teaspoon baking powder
125 g (4¹/₂ oz/1 cup) roughly chopped pecans

1   Preheat the oven to 180°C (350°F/Gas 4). Grease a 17 cm (6¹/₂ inch) square tin and line the base with baking paper, leaving it hanging over two opposite sides.

2   Place the chocolate in a heatproof bowl. Bring a saucepan of water to the boil and remove from the heat. Sit the bowl over the pan— ensure the bowl doesn't touch the water. Stand, stirring occasionally, until melted. Cool slightly.

3   Beat the butter, sugar and vanilla extract with electric beaters until thick and creamy. Beat in the eggs one at a time, beating well after each addition. Stir in the melted chocolate.

4   Fold in the sifted combined flour, cocoa and baking powder with a metal spoon, then fold in the pecans. Spoon into the prepared tin and smooth the surface. Bake for 30–35 minutes, or until the mixture is firm and comes away from the side of the tin. Cool in the tin, remove and cut into squares.

Wholemeal Apricot Slice

Makes 15 pieces

200 g (7 oz) unsalted butter
115 g (4 oz/¹/2 cup) caster (superfine) sugar
125 g (4¹/2 oz/1 cup) plain (all-purpose) flour
125 g (4¹/2 oz/1 cup) wholemeal (whole-wheat) self-raising flour

FILLING
200 g (7 oz/1 heaped cup) dried apricots, finely chopped
2 teaspoons honey

1 Preheat the oven to 180°C (350°F/Gas 4). Brush a 27 x 18 cm
   (10³/4 x 7 inch) shallow baking tin with melted butter or oil. Line the
   tin with baking paper, leaving it hanging over two sides.

2 Using electric beaters, cream the butter and sugar until light and
   fluffy. Add the sifted flours and mix to a soft dough. Place two-thirds
   of the dough in the prepared tin and smooth the surface with the
   back of a spoon.

3 To make the filling, combine the apricots, honey and 185 ml (6 fl oz/
   ³/4 cup) water in a small saucepan. Stir over medium heat until the
   mixture starts to boil. Reduce the heat and simmer for 5 minutes, or
   until the liquid has evaporated. Allow to cool.

4 Spread the filling onto the pastry base. Crumble the remaining dough
   through your fingers and sprinkle over the top. Bake for 25 minutes,
   or until golden. Cool and cut into squares.

Peppermint Slice

Makes 15 pieces

85 g (3 oz/²/3 cup) self-raising flour
60 g (2¹/4 oz/¹/2 cup) plain (all-purpose) flour
30 g (1 oz/¹/4 cup) unsweetened cocoa powder
115 g (4 oz/¹/2 cup) caster (superfine) sugar
1 egg, lightly beaten
125 g (4¹/2 oz) unsalted butter, melted

MINT FILLING
60 ml (2 fl oz/¹/4 cup) pouring (whipping) cream
2 teaspoons vegetable oil
1 tablespoon liquid glucose
250 g (9 oz/2 cups) icing (confectioners') sugar, sifted
natural peppermint extract

ICING
100 g (3¹/2 oz/²/3 cup) chopped dark chocolate
1 tablespoon pouring (whipping) cream
40 g (1¹/2 oz) unsalted butter

1 Preheat the oven to 180°C (350°F/Gas 4). Line the base and side of a shallow 27 x 18 cm (10³/4 x 7 inch) baking tin with foil.

2 Sift the flours, cocoa and sugar into a bowl. Make a well in the centre. Pour in the combined egg and butter. Using a wooden spoon, stir until well combined. Press the mixture evenly into the prepared tin. Bake for 15–20 minutes, or until skewer comes out clean when inserted into the centre of the slice. Allow to cool in the tin.

3 To make the mint filling, combine the cream, oil, glucose and icing sugar in a heavy-based saucepan. Stir over low heat until the mixture is smooth and creamy. Add a few drops of peppermint extract and mix well. Remove from the heat. Pour the mixture onto the base of the slice and smooth the surface with a flat-bladed knife. Allow to set.

4 To make the icing, combine the chocolate, cream and butter in a small saucepan over low heat, stirring well. Using a flat-bladed knife, carefully spread over the slice and allow to set completely before cutting and serving.

Poppy Seed Slice

Makes 14 pieces

125 g (4¹/2 oz/1 cup) plain (all-purpose) flour
75 g (2¹/2 oz) unsalted butter, chilled and cubed
60 g (2¹/4 oz/¹/4 cup) caster (superfine) sugar
1 egg yolk
40 g (1¹/2 oz/¹/4 cup) poppy seeds
2 tablespoons warm milk
125 g (4¹/2 oz) unsalted butter, extra
90 g (3¹/4 oz/¹/3 cup) caster (superfine) sugar, extra
1 teaspoon finely grated lemon zest
1 egg, extra
90 g (3¹/4 oz/³/4 cup) plain (all-purpose) flour, extra, sifted
125 g (4¹/2 oz/1 cup) icing (confectioners') sugar
¹/2 teaspoon finely grated lemon zest, extra
1 tablespoon lemon juice

1   Preheat the oven to 180°C (350°F/Gas 4). Grease an 11 x 35 cm
    (4¹/4 x 14 inch) loose-based flan (tart) tin. Sift the flour into a
    bowl and rub in the butter with your fingertips until it resembles
    breadcrumbs. Stir in the sugar. Make a well in the centre and then
    add 2–3 teaspoons water and the egg yolk. Mix with a flat-bladed knife,
    using a cutting action until it comes together in beads. Press into a ball
    and flatten slightly. Cover with plastic wrap and chill for 15 minutes.

2   Roll out the dough to fit the base and sides of the prepared tin. Trim the
    edges. Cover the base and sides of the pastry shell with a piece
    of crumpled baking paper. Pour in some baking beads, dried beans or
    uncooked rice. Blind bake the pastry for 10 minutes, then remove the
    paper and beads and bake for 5 minutes, or until the pastry is dry. Cool.

3   Soak the poppy seeds in the milk for 10 minutes. Cream the extra butter, extra sugar and lemon zest until light and fluffy. Beat in the extra egg and stir in the poppy seed mixture and extra flour. Spread over the pastry base and bake for 25 minutes, or until light brown. Cool in the tin until warm.

4   Combine the icing sugar, extra lemon zest and enough lemon juice to form a paste. Spread over the slice and cool.

Chocolate Truffle Macaroon Slice

Makes 24 pieces

3 egg whites
185 g (6¹/2 oz/heaped ³/4 cup) caster (superfine) sugar
180 g (6 oz/2 cups) desiccated coconut
250 g (9 oz/1²/3 cups) chopped dark chocolate
300 ml (10¹/2 fl oz/1¹/4 cups) pouring (whipping) cream
1 tablespoon unsweetened cocoa powder

1 Preheat the oven to 180°C (350°F/Gas 4). Lightly grease a 20 x 30 cm (8 x 12 inch) shallow baking tin and line with baking paper, leaving it hanging over the two long sides.

2 Beat the egg whites in a clean, dry bowl until soft peaks form. Slowly add the sugar, beating well after each addition until stiff and glossy. Fold in the coconut. Spread into the prepared tin and bake for 20 minutes, or until light brown. While still warm, press down lightly but firmly with a palette knife. Cool completely.

3 Place the chocolate in a heatproof bowl. Bring a saucepan of water to the boil, then remove from the heat. Sit the bowl over the pan— ensure the bowl doesn't touch the water. Stand, stirring occasionally, until the chocolate has melted. Cool slightly.

4 Whip the cream until thick. Gently fold in the chocolate until well combined—do not overmix or it will curdle. Spread evenly over the coconut base and refrigerate for 3 hours, or until set. Carefully lift from the tin and dust with the cocoa.

Sesame and Ginger Slice

Makes 15 pieces

125 g (4¹/₂ oz/1 cup) plain (all-purpose) flour
¹/₂ teaspoon bicarbonate of soda (baking soda)
1 teaspoon ground ginger
¹/₄ teaspoon mixed (pumpkin pie) spice
2 eggs
140 g (5 oz/³/₄ cup) soft brown sugar
125 g (4¹/₂ oz) unsalted butter, melted
55 g (2 oz/¹/₄ cup) glacé (candied) ginger, chopped
50 g (1³/₄ oz/¹/₃ cup) sesame seeds, toasted

1   Preheat the oven to 180°C (350°F/Gas 4). Lightly grease a 20 x 30 cm
    (8 x 12 inch) shallow baking tin and line with baking paper, leaving it
    hanging over the two long sides.

2   Sift together the flour, bicarbonate of soda, ginger, mixed spice and
    ¹/₄ teaspoon salt. Beat the eggs and sugar in a large bowl for 2 minutes,
    or until thick and creamy. Mix in the butter and gently fold in the
    flour mixture. Add the glacé ginger and half the sesame seeds and
    mix gently.

3   Spread into the prepared tin and sprinkle with the remaining sesame
    seeds. Bake for 20 minutes, or until firm to touch and slightly
    coloured. Cool in the tin for 10 minutes, then cool on a wire rack.

apple pie portuguese custard tarts mini éclai

Pastries, tarts and pies

Apple Pie

Makes 1

FILLING

6 large granny smith apples, peeled and cored

2 tablespoons caster (superfine) sugar

1 teaspoon finely grated lemon zest

pinch of ground cloves

250 g (9 oz/2 cups) plain (all-purpose) flour

30 g (1 oz/^{1}/4 cup) self-raising flour

150 g (5^1/2 oz) unsalted butter, chilled and cubed

2 tablespoons caster (superfine) sugar

4–5 tablespoons iced water

2 tablespoons marmalade

1 egg, lightly beaten

1 tablespoon sugar

1   Lightly grease a 23 cm (9 inch) pie dish. Cut the apples into wedges. Place in a saucepan with the sugar, lemon zest, cloves and 2 tablespoons water. Cover and cook over low heat for 8 minutes, or until the apples are just tender, shaking the pan occasionally. Drain and cool completely.

2   Sift the flours into a bowl and rub in the butter, using your fingertips, until the mixture resembles fine breadcrumbs. Stir in the sugar, then make a well in the centre. Add almost all the iced water and mix with a flat-bladed knife, using a cutting action, until the mixture comes together in beads. Add more iced water if the dough is too dry. Gather together and lift out onto a lightly floured surface. Press into a ball and divide into two, making one half a little bigger. Cover with plastic wrap and refrigerate for 20 minutes.

3 Preheat the oven to 200°C (400°F/Gas 6). Roll out the larger piece of pastry between two sheets of baking paper to line the base and side of the pie dish. Line the pie dish with the pastry. Use a small sharp knife to trim away any excess pastry. Brush the marmalade over the base and spoon the apple into the case.

4 Roll out the remaining pastry between the baking paper until large enough to cover the pie. Brush water around the rim, then place the top on. Trim off any excess pastry, pinch the edges and cut a round hole or a couple of steam slits in the top.

5 Re-roll the pastry scraps and cut into leaves for decoration. Lightly brush the top with the egg, then sprinkle with the sugar. Bake for 20 minutes, then reduce the oven temperature to 180°C (350°F/Gas 4) and bake for another 15–20 minutes, or until golden.

 The secret to making good shortcrust pastry is to work quickly and lightly, in a cool room if possible, on a cool surface.

Custard Tarts

Makes 12

250 g (9 oz/2 cups) plain (all-purpose) flour
60 g (2¼ oz/⅓ cup) rice flour
30 g (1 oz/¼ cup) icing (confectioners') sugar
120 g (4¼ oz) unsalted butter, chilled and cubed
1 egg yolk
3 tablespoons iced water
1 egg white, lightly beaten

CUSTARD FILLING
3 eggs
375 ml (13 fl oz/1½ cups) milk
60 g (2¼ oz/¼ cup) caster (superfine) sugar
1 teaspoon natural vanilla extract
½ teaspoon ground nutmeg

1 Sift the flours and icing sugar into a large bowl and rub in the butter, using your fingertips, until the mixture resembles fine breadcrumbs. Make a well in the centre and add the egg yolk and almost all the water. Mix with a flat-bladed knife, using a cutting action, until the mixture comes together in small beads, adding more iced water if the dough is too dry.

2 Gather the pastry together and roll out between two sheets of baking paper. Divide the dough into 12 equal portions and roll each portion out to fit the base and side of twelve 10 cm (4 inch) loose-based fluted tartlet tins. Line the tins with the pastry and roll the rolling pin over the tins to cut off any excess pastry. Refrigerate for 20 minutes.

3 Preheat the oven to 180°C (350°F/Gas 4). Line each pastry case with crumpled baking paper. Fill with baking beads, dried beans or uncooked rice. Place the tins on two large baking trays and bake for 10 minutes. Remove the baking paper and beads and return the trays to the oven. Bake for 10 minutes, or until the pastry is lightly golden. Cool. Brush the base and side of each pastry case with beaten egg white. Reduce the oven temperature to 150°C (300°F/Gas 2).

4 To make the custard filling, whisk the eggs and milk in a bowl to combine. Add the sugar gradually, whisking to dissolve completely. Stir in the vanilla extract. Strain into a jug, then pour into the cooled pastry cases. Sprinkle with the nutmeg and bake for 25 minutes, or until the filling is just set. Serve at room temperature.

Fig Shortcake

Serves 12

185 g (6¹/2 oz/1¹/2 cups) plain (all-purpose) flour
60 g (2¹/4 oz/¹/2 cup) self-raising flour
2 teaspoons ground cinnamon
1 teaspoon ground ginger
1 teaspoon mixed (pumpkin pie) spice
115 g (4 oz/¹/2 cup) soft brown sugar
55 g (2 oz/¹/2 cup) ground hazelnuts
125 g (4¹/2 oz) unsalted butter, cubed
1 egg, lightly beaten
315 g (11¹/4 oz/1 cup) fig jam
95 g (3¹/2 oz/²/3 cup) hazelnuts, toasted and finely chopped
icing (confectioners') sugar, to dust

1 Preheat the oven to 180°C (350°F/Gas 4). Grease a 35 x 11 cm (14 x 4¹/4 inch) loose-based rectangular shallow flan (tart) tin.

2 Combine the flours, spices, sugar and ground hazelnuts in a food processor and process to just combine. Add the butter and, using the pulse button, process in short bursts until crumbly. Add the egg, a little at a time, until the mixture comes together; you may not need all the egg. Divide the dough in half, wrap separately in plastic wrap and refrigerate for 30 minutes.

3 Remove one ball of dough from the refrigerator and roll out between two sheets of baking paper, large enough to fit the base and side of the tin. Ease the pastry into the prepared tin, gently pressing to fit into the corners, and patching any holes with extra dough, if necessary. Trim away the excess.

4 Spread the pastry with the fig jam. Coarsley grate the second chilled
ball of dough into a bowl, add the chopped hazelnuts and gently toss
to combine. Press the mixture gently over the top of the jam, taking
care to retain the grated texture. Bake for 35 minutes, or until golden
brown. Cool completely in the tin before cutting, and dust lightly
with icing sugar. Serve with whipped cream, if desired.

 Fig shortcake will keep, stored in an
airtight container, for up to 4 days, or
up to 3 months in the freezer.

Mini Eclairs

Makes 24

60 g (2¹/4 oz) unsalted butter, cubed
125 g (4¹/2 oz/1 cup) plain (all-purpose) flour, sifted
4 eggs, beaten
50 g (1³/4 oz/¹/3 cup) chopped dark chocolate

FILLING
300 ml (10¹/2 fl oz/1¹/4 cups) pouring (whipping) cream
1 tablespoon icing (confectioners') sugar, sifted
¹/2 teaspoon natural vanilla extract

1 Preheat the oven to 200°C (400°F/Gas 6) and line two baking trays
with baking paper.

2 To make choux pastry, put the butter in a saucepan with 250 ml
(9 fl oz/1 cup) water. Stir over low heat until melted. Bring to the boil,
then remove from the heat and add all the flour. Beat with a wooden
spoon until smooth. Return to the heat and beat for 2 minutes, or until
the mixture forms a ball and leaves the side of the pan.

3 Remove from the heat and transfer to a bowl. Cool for 5 minutes.
Add the egg, a little at a time, beating well after each addition, until
thick and glossy—a wooden spoon should stand upright.

4 Spoon into a piping bag with a 1.2 cm (¹/2 inch) plain nozzle. Pipe 6 cm
(2¹/2 inch) lengths of pastry batter on the prepared trays. Bake
for 10 minutes, then reduce the oevn temperature to 180°C (350°F/
Gas 4) and cook for 10 minutes, or until golden and puffed. Poke a hole
into one side of each éclair and remove the soft dough from inside with
a teaspoon. Return to the oven for 3 minutes to dry out. Cool on a rack.

5 Place the chocolate in a heatproof bowl. Bring a saucepan of water to the boil, then remove from the heat. Sit the bowl over the saucepan of water—make sure the bowl doesn't touch the water. Leave the chocolate to soften a little, then stir until smooth and melted.

6 To make the filling, whip the cream, icing sugar and vanilla extract until thick. Pipe the cream into the side of each éclair. Dip each éclair into the melted chocolate, top side down, then return to the wire rack for the chocolate to set.

Pear and Almond Flan

Serves 8

155 g (5 1/2 oz/1 1/4 cups) plain (all-purpose) flour
90 g (3 1/4 oz) unsalted butter, chilled and cubed
60 g (2 1/4 oz/1/4 cup) caster (superfine) sugar
2 egg yolks, lightly beaten

FILLING
165 g (5 3/4 oz) unsalted butter, softened
160 g (5 1/2 oz/3/4 cup) caster (superfine) sugar
3 eggs
135 g (4 3/4 oz/1 1/3 cups) ground almonds
1 1/2 tablespoons plain (all-purpose) flour
2 very ripe pears

1   Lightly grease a shallow 24 cm (9 1/2 inch) round, loose-based, fluted
flan (tart) tin. Sift the flour into a bowl and rub in the butter, using
your fingertips, until the mixture resembles fine breadcrumbs. Stir in
the sugar and mix together. Make a well in the centre, add the egg
yolk and mix with a flat-bladed knife, using a cutting action, until the
mixture comes together in beads. Turn out onto a lightly floured
surface and gather into a ball. Wrap in plastic wrap and refrigerate
for 30 minutes.

2   Preheat the oven to 180°C (350°F/Gas 4). Roll out the pastry between
two sheets of baking paper until large enough to line the base and side
of the tin. Ease the pastry into the tin and trim off any excess. Sparsely
prick the base with a fork. Line the base with baking paper, pour in some
baking beads, dried beans or uncooked rice and bake for 10 minutes.
Remove the paper and beads and bake for another 10 minutes. Cool.

3   To make the filling, beat the butter and sugar in a bowl with electric beaters for 30 seconds (don't cream the mixture). Add the eggs one at a time, beating after each addition. Fold in the ground almonds and flour and spread the filling smoothly over the cooled pastry base.

4   Peel the pears, halve lengthways and remove the cores. Cut crossways into 3 mm (1/8 inch) slices. Separate the slices slightly, then place each half on top of the tart to form a cross. Bake for 50 minutes, or until the filling has set (the middle may still be a little soft). Cool in the tin, then refrigerate for at least 2 hours before serving. Dust with icing (confectioners') sugar if you wish.

Portuguese Custard Tarts

Makes 12

155 g (5¹/2 oz/1¹/4 cups) plain (all-purpose) flour
25 g (1 oz) Copha (white vegetable shortening), cubed and softened
30 g (1 oz) unsalted butter, cubed and softened
250 g (9 oz/1 heaped cup) sugar
500 ml (17 fl oz/2 cups) milk
3 tablespoons cornflour (cornstarch)
1 tablespoon custard powder (instant vanilla pudding mix)
4 egg yolks
1 teaspoon natural vanilla extract

1   Sift the flour into a bowl. Add 185 ml (6 fl oz/³/4 cup) water, or enough to form a soft dough. Gather into a ball, then roll out on a sheet of baking paper to form a 24 x 30 cm (9¹/2 x 12 inch) rectangle. Spread the Copha over the surface. Roll up from the short edge to form a log.

2   Roll the dough out into a rectangle again, and spread with the butter. Roll into a log and slice into 12 pieces.

3   Working from the centre outwards, use your fingertips to press each round out to a circle large enough to cover the base and side of twelve 80 ml (2¹/2 fl oz/¹/3 cup) muffin holes. Press into the tin and refrigerate.

4   Put the sugar and 80 ml (2¹/2 fl oz/¹/3 cup) water into a saucepan, and stir over low heat until the sugar dissolves. Mix a little milk with the cornflour and custard powder to form a smooth paste, and add to the pan with the remaining milk, egg yolks and vanilla extract. Stir over low heat until thickened. Put in a bowl, cover and cool.

5 Preheat the oven to 220°C (425°F/Gas 7). Divide the filling among the pastry cases. Bake for 30 minutes, or until the custard is set and the tops have browned. Cool in the tins, then transfer to a wire rack.

Lemon Meringue Pie

Serves 6

185 g (6¹/₂ oz/1¹/₂ cups) plain (all-purpose) flour
125 g (4¹/₂ oz) unsalted butter, chilled and cubed
2 tablespoons icing (confectioners') sugar
2–3 tablespoons iced water

LEMON FILLING
30 g (1 oz/¹/₄ cup) cornflour (cornstarch)
30 g (1 oz/¹/₄ cup) plain (all-purpose) flour
250 g (9 oz/1 heaped cup) caster (superfine) sugar
185 ml (6 fl oz/³/₄ cup) lemon juice
3 teaspoons grated lemon zest
40 g (1¹/₂ oz) unsalted butter
6 egg yolks

MERINGUE TOPPING
6 egg whites
375 g (13 oz/1²/₃ cups) caster (superfine) sugar
¹/₂ teaspoon cornflour (cornstarch)

1   Lightly grease a deep 23 cm (9 inch) pie dish. Sift the flour into a bowl and rub in the butter, using your fingertips, until the mixture resembles fine breadcrumbs. Stir in the icing sugar, then make a well in the centre. Add 2 tablespoons of the iced water and mix with a flat-bladed knife, using a cutting action, until the mixture comes together in beads. Add the remaining iced water if the dough is too dry.

2   Roll the dough between two sheets of baking paper until large enough to line the base and side of the pie dish. Line the dish with the pastry. Trim off any excess. Seal the edges with a fork and chill for 15 minutes.

3 Preheat the oven to 180°C (350°F/Gas 4). Line the pastry case with crumpled baking paper and pour in some baking beads, dried beans or uncooked rice. Bake for 10–15 minutes, then remove the paper and beads. Return the pastry to the oven for 10 minutes, or until cooked through. Cool completely. Increase the oven temperature to 220°C (425°F/Gas 7).

4 To make the lemon filling, put the flours and sugar in a saucepan. Whisk in the lemon juice, zest and 375 ml (13 fl oz/1$^{1}/_{2}$ cups) water. Whisk constantly over medium heat until the mixture boils and thickens, then reduce the heat and cook for 1 minute. Remove from the heat, then whisk in the butter, then the egg yolks, one at a time. Cover the surface with plastic wrap and set aside to cool. Spread the cooled filling into the pastry case.

5 To make the meringue topping, put the egg whites and sugar in a clean, dry bowl. Beat with electric beaters on high for 10 minutes, or until the sugar is almost completely dissolved and the meringue is thick and glossy. Beat in the cornflour. Spread the meringue over the filling, making peaks by drawing the meringue up with a knife, piling it high towards the centre. Bake for 5–10 minutes, or until lightly browned. Cool before serving.

Baklava

Makes 16 pieces

375 g (13 oz/3 cups) walnuts, finely chopped
155 g (5½ oz/1 cup) almonds, finely chopped
½ teaspoon ground cinnamon
½ teaspoon mixed (pumpkin pie) spice
1 tablespoon caster (superfine) sugar
16 sheets ready-made filo pastry
1 tablespoon olive oil
200 g (7 oz) unsalted butter, melted

SYRUP
500 g (1 lb 2 oz/2¼ cups) sugar
3 whole cloves
3 teaspoons lemon juice

1   Preheat the oven to 180°C (350°F/Gas 4). Lightly grease the base
    and side of an 18 x 28 cm (7 x 11¼ inch) shallow baking tin.

2   Mix together the walnuts, almonds, spices and sugar, then divide into
    three portions. Work with one sheet of filo pastry at a time, keeping
    the rest covered with a damp tea (dish) towel to prevent drying out.
    Place a sheet of pastry on a work surface. Mix the oil and melted
    butter together and brush liberally over the pastry sheet. Fold the
    sheet in half crossways. Trim the edges so the pastry fits the base of
    the prepared tin. Repeat with another 3 sheets of pastry, brushing
    each layer liberally with the butter mixture.

3   Sprinkle one portion of the nut filling over the pastry. Continue
    buttering the pastry, 4 sheets at a time as before, and layering with
    the nuts. Finish with pastry on top.

4 Trim the edges and brush the top with the remaining butter and oil. Score the slice lengthways into four even portions and bake for 30 minutes, or until golden and crisp.

5 To make the syrup, put the sugar, cloves, lemon juice and 330 ml (11¼ fl oz/1⅓ cups) water in a small saucepan and stir over low heat, without boiling, until the sugar has dissolved. Bring to the boil, then reduce the heat and simmer, without stirring, for 10 minutes, or until thickened. Remove from the heat and set aside to cool.

6 When the baklava is cooked, pour the cooled syrup over the hot slice. The syrup should have the consistency of thick honey and will take a little while to soak in. Leave to cool and cut into diamonds when cold.

 Baklava can be stored in a cool place in an airtight container for up to 5 days.

Butter Almond Torte

Serves 8–10

120 g (4$^{1}/_{4}$ oz) unsalted butter, cubed
90 ml (3 fl oz) milk
2 eggs
1 teaspoon natural vanilla extract
250 g (9 oz/1 heaped cup) caster (superfine) sugar
135 g (4$^{3}/_{4}$ oz/1 heaped cup) plain (all-purpose) flour
2 teaspoons baking powder
100 g (3$^{1}/_{2}$ oz/$^{3}/_{4}$ cup) slivered almonds

1 Preheat the oven to 180°C (350°F/Gas 4). Line the base of a 22 cm (8$^{1}/_{2}$ inch) spring-form cake tin with foil and lightly grease the base and side.

2 Heat 60 g (2$^{1}/_{4}$ oz) of the butter and 80 ml (2$^{1}/_{2}$ fl oz/$^{1}/_{3}$ cup) of the milk in a small saucepan until the butter has melted.

3 Beat the eggs, vanilla extract and 185 g (6$^{1}/_{2}$ oz/$^{3}/_{4}$ cup) of the sugar with electric beaters until thick and creamy. Stir in the butter and milk mixture. Sift in 125 g (4$^{1}/_{2}$ oz/1 cup) of the flour and the baking powder and stir to combine—the mixture will be thin. Pour into the prepared tin and bake for 50 minutes.

4 Melt the remaining butter in a small saucepan. Stir in the almonds with the remaining sugar, flour and milk and stir until combined. Quickly spoon the topping onto the cake (the centre will still be uncooked), starting from the outside edges; avoid piling the topping in the centre. Return to the oven for a further 10–15 minutes, or until the topping is golden and the torte is cooked through. Cool in the tin before inverting onto a wire rack.

Jam Roly Poly

Serves 4

250 g (9 oz/2 cups) self-raising flour, sifted
125 g (4¹/2 oz) unsalted butter, chilled and cubed
2 tablespoons caster (superfine) sugar
50 ml (1³/4 fl oz) milk
210 g (7¹/2 oz/²/3 cup) raspberry jam
1 tablespoon milk, extra

1   Preheat the oven to 180°C (350°F/Gas 4) and line a baking tray with baking paper. Sift the flour into a large bowl and rub in the butter, using your fingertips, until the mixture resembles fine breadcrumbs. Stir in the sugar and make a well in the centre.

2   Add the milk and 50 ml (1³/4 fl oz) water to the well in the flour and mix with a flat-bladed knife, using a cutting action, until the mixture comes together in beads. Turn out onto a lightly floured surface and gather together to form a smooth dough. Roll out the dough, on a sheet of baking paper, into a rectangle measuring about 33 x 23 cm (13 x 9 inches) and 5 mm (¹/4 inch) thick. Spread with the raspberry jam, leaving a 5 mm (¹/4 inch) border all around.

3   Roll up the dough lengthways like a swiss (jelly) roll and place on the prepared tray, seam side down. Brush with the extra milk and bake for 35 minutes, or until golden and cooked through. Leave for a few minutes before cutting into thick slices with a serrated knife. Serve warm with custard if you wish.

During cooking, the jam will ooze out slightly from the pastry but this is fine.

Chocolate Fudge Pecan Pie

Serves 6

155 g (5¹/2 oz/1¹/4 cups) plain (all-purpose) flour
2 tablespoons unsweetened cocoa powder
2 tablespoons soft brown sugar
100 g (3¹/2 oz) unsalted butter, chilled and cubed
2–3 tablespoons iced water

FILLING
200 g (7 oz/1²/3 cups) pecans, roughly chopped
100 g (3¹/2 oz/²/3 cup) chopped dark chocolate
95 g (3¹/4 oz/¹/2 cup) soft brown sugar
170 ml (5¹/2 fl oz/²/3 cup) light or dark corn syrup
3 eggs, lightly beaten
2 teaspoons natural vanilla extract

1 Grease a 23 x 18 x 3 cm (9 x 7 x 1¹/4 inch) pie dish. Sift the flour, cocoa and sugar into a bowl and rub in the butter, using your fingertips, until the mixture resembles fine breadcrumbs. Make a well in the centre, add almost all the iced water and mix with a knife, adding more water if necessary.

2 Gather the dough together and lift onto a sheet of baking paper. Press the dough out into a disc and refrigerate for 20 minutes. Roll out the pastry between two sheets of baking paper to fit the pie dish. Ease the pastry into the dish and trim the edges. Chill for 20 minutes.

3 Preheat the oven to 180°C (350°F/Gas 4). Cover the pastry with crumpled baking paper and fill with baking beads, dried beans or uncooked rice. Bake for 15 minutes, then remove the paper and beads and bake for 15–20 minutes, or until the base is dry. Cool.

4   Place the pie dish on a flat baking tray to catch any drips. To make
    the filling, spread the pecans and chocolate over the pastry base.
    Combine the sugar, corn syrup, eggs and vanilla extract in a jug and
    whisk together with a fork. Pour into the pastry case, and bake for
    45 minutes (the filling will still be a bit wobbly, but will set on
    cooling). Cool before cutting to serve.

Apple Tarte Tatin

Serves 6

210 g (7^1/2 oz/1^2/3 cups) plain (all-purpose) flour
125 g (4^1/2 oz) unsalted butter, chilled and cubed
2 tablespoons caster (superfine) sugar
1 egg, lightly beaten
2 drops natural vanilla extract
8 granny smith apples, peeled and cored
125 g (4^1/2 oz/^{2}/3 cup) sugar
40 g (1^1/2 oz) unsalted butter, cubed, extra

1   Sift the flour into a bowl and rub in the butter, using your fingertips, until the mixture resembles fine breadcrumbs. Stir in the caster sugar, then make a well in the centre. Add the egg and vanilla extract and mix with a flat-bladed knife, using a cutting action, until the mixture comes together in beads. Gather the dough together, then turn out onto a lightly floured surface and shape into a disc. Wrap in plastic wrap and refrigerate for at least 30 minutes, to firm.

2   Cut each apple into eight slices. Place the sugar and 1 tablespoon water in a heavy-based 25 cm (10 inch) ovenproof frying pan. Stir over low heat for 1 minute, or until the sugar has dissolved. Increase the heat to medium and cook for 4–5 minutes, or until the caramel turns golden. Add the extra butter and stir. Remove from the heat.

3   Place the apple slices in neat circles to cover the base of the frying pan. Return the pan to low heat and cook for 10–12 minutes, until the apples are tender and caramelized. Remove from the heat and leave to cool for 10 minutes.

4 Preheat the oven to 220°C (425°F/Gas 7). Roll the pastry out on a lightly floured surface to a circle 1 cm (¹/₂ inch) larger than the frying pan. Place the pastry over the apples to cover them completely, tucking it down firmly at the edges. Bake for 30–35 minutes, or until the pastry is cooked. Leave for 15 minutes before turning out onto a plate. Serve warm or cold with cream or ice cream if you wish.

Special high-sided tatin tins are available for making this dessert. Look for them at speciality kitchenware shops.

Date and Mascarpone Tart

Serves 6–8

90 g (3¹/4 oz/¹/2 cup) rice flour
60 g (2¹/4 oz/¹/2 cup) plain (all-purpose) flour
100 g (3¹/2 oz) unsalted butter, chilled and cubed
2 tablespoons icing (confectioners') sugar
25 g (1 oz/¹/4 cup) desiccated coconut
100 g (3¹/2 oz) marzipan, grated

FILLING
8 fresh dates, pitted
2 eggs
2 teaspoons custard powder (instant vanilla pudding mix)
125 g (4¹/2 oz/heaped ¹/2 cup) mascarpone cheese
2 tablespoons caster (superfine) sugar
80 ml (2¹/2 fl oz/¹/3 cup) pouring (whipping) cream
2 tablespoons flaked almonds

1   Preheat the oven to 180°C (350°F/Gas 4). Grease a shallow
    10 x 34 cm (4 x 13¹/2 inch) fluted loose-bottomed flan (tart) tin.

2   Sift the flours into a large bowl. Using just your fingertips, rub in
    the butter until the mixture resembles breadcrumbs. Stir in the icing
    sugar, coconut and marzipan, then press the mixture together gently.
    Turn out onto a lightly floured surface and gather together into
    a ball. Flatten slightly, cover with plastic wrap and refrigerate for
    15 minutes.

3 Roll out the pastry between two sheets of baking paper until large
   enough to line the tin. Ease the pastry into the tin and trim the edge.
   Refrigerate for 5–10 minutes. Line the pastry case with a crumpled
   sheet of baking paper and fill with baking beads, dried beans or
   uncooked rice. Place the tin on a baking tray and bake for 10 minutes.
   Remove the paper and beads, bake for another 5 minutes, or until just
   golden, then allow to cool.

4 To make the filling, cut the dates into quarters lengthways and
   arrange over the pastry. Whisk together the eggs, custard powder,
   mascarpone, sugar and cream until smooth. Pour the mixture
   over the dates, then sprinkle with the flaked almonds. Bake for
   25–30 minutes, or until golden and just set, then allow to cool
   slightly. Serve warm.

Sugar and Spice Palmiers

Makes 32

500 g (1 lb 2 oz) ready-made puff pastry
2 tablespoons sugar
1 teaspoon mixed (pumpkin pie) spice
1 teaspoon ground cinnamon
40 g (1½ oz) unsalted butter, melted
icing (confectioners') sugar, to dust

1   Preheat the oven to 210°C (415°F/Gas 6–7). Lightly grease two baking trays, then line with baking paper. Roll out the pastry between two sheets of baking paper to make a 30 cm (12 inch) square 3 mm (⅛ inch) thick. Combine the sugar and spices in a small bowl. Cut the sheet of pastry in half, then brush each pastry sheet with melted butter. Sprinkle with the sugar mixture, reserving 2 teaspoons.

2   Fold the short edges of pastry inwards, so that the edges almost meet in the centre. Fold the same way once more, then fold over and place both rolls on a tray. Refrigerate for 15 minutes. Using a small, sharp knife, cut into 32 slices.

3   Arrange the palmiers, cut side up, on the baking trays; brush with butter and sprinkle lightly with the reserved sugar mixture. Bake for 20 minutes, or until golden. Leave to cool on a wire rack. Lightly dust with sifted icing sugar before serving.

Palmiers can be stored for up to a day in an airtight container. If you wish, you can re-crisp them in the oven at 180°C (350°F/Gas 4) for 5 minutes.

Banana and Plum Crumble

Serves 4-6

30 g (1 oz/^{1}/4 cup) plain (all-purpose) flour
50 g (1^3/4 oz/^{1}/2 cup) rolled (porridge) oats
30 g (1 oz/^{1}/2 cup) shredded coconut
45 g (1^1/2 oz/^{1}/4 cup) soft brown sugar
finely grated zest of 1 lime
100 g (3^1/2 oz) unsalted butter, cubed
2 bananas, peeled and halved lengthways
4 plums, halved and stoned
60 ml (2 fl oz/^{1}/4 cup) lime juice

1   Preheat the oven to 180°C (350°F/Gas 4). Combine the flour, rolled oats, coconut, sugar and lime zest in a small bowl. Add the butter and, using your fingertips, rub the butter into the flour mixture until crumbly.

2   Put the bananas and plums in a 1.25 litre (44 fl oz/5 cup) capacity ovenproof dish and pour the lime juice over. Turn to coat in the juice.

3   Sprinkle the crumble mixture evenly over the fruit. Bake for 25–30 minutes, or until the crumble is golden. Serve hot with ice cream or whipped cream.

Lemon Almond Tart

250 g (9 oz/2 cups) plain (all-purpose) flour, sifted
60 g (2¼ oz/¼ cup) caster (superfine) sugar
125 g (4½ oz) unsalted butter, softened
1 teaspoon finely grated lemon zest
2 egg yolks

FILLING
350 g (12 oz/1½ cups) ricotta cheese, sieved
90 g (3¼ oz/⅓ cup) caster (superfine) sugar
3 eggs, well beaten
1 tablespoon finely grated lemon zest
80 g (2¾ oz/½ cup) blanched almonds, finely chopped
3 tablespoons flaked almonds
icing (confectioners') sugar, to dust

1   Combine the flour, sugar and a pinch of salt in a large bowl. Make a
well in the centre and add the butter, lemon zest and egg yolks. Work
the flour into the centre with the fingertips of one hand until a
smooth dough forms (add a little more flour if necessary). Wrap in
plastic wrap, flatten slightly, then refrigerate for 20 minutes.

2   To make the filling, beat the ricotta and sugar together with electric
beaters. Add the eggs gradually, beating well after each addition.
Add the lemon zest, beating briefly to combine, then stir in the
chopped almonds.

3 Preheat the oven to 180°C (350°F/Gas 4). Brush a 20 cm (8 inch) fluted flan (tart) tin with melted butter. Roll out the pastry on a lightly floured surface and ease it the tin, trimming away any excess pastry. Pour in the filling and smooth the top. Sprinkle with the flaked almonds and bake for 55 minutes to 1 hour, or until lightly golden and set.

4 Cool to room temperature, then carefully remove the sides from the tin. Lightly dust with icing sugar and serve chilled or at room temperature.

Nutty Fig Pie

Serves 8

375 g (13 oz) ready-made sweet shortcrust pie pastry
200 g (7 oz/1½ cups) hazelnuts
100 g (3½ oz/⅔ cup) pine nuts
100 g (3½ oz/1 cup) flaked almonds
100 g (3½ oz/⅔ cup) blanched almonds
170 ml (5½ fl oz/⅔ cup) pouring (whipping) cream
60 g (2¼ oz) unsalted butter
90 g (3¼ oz/¼ cup) honey
95 g (3¼ oz/½ cup) soft brown sugar
150 g (5½ oz/1 cup) dried figs, cut into quarters

1 Preheat the oven to 200°C (400°F/Gas 6) and grease a 23 x 18 x 3 cm
(9 x 7 x 1¼ inch) pie dish. Roll the pastry out until large enough to
cover the base and side of the dish. Remove the top sheet and invert
the pastry into the dish, allowing any excess to hang over. Trim with a
knife and prick the base several times with a fork. Score the edge with a
fork. Refrigerate for 20 minutes, then bake for 15 minutes, or until
lightly golden. Allow to cool.

2 Place the hazelnuts on a baking tray and bake for 8 minutes, or until the
skins start to peel away. Tip into a tea (dish) towel and rub to remove
the skins. Place the pine nuts, flaked almonds and blanched almonds on
a baking tray and bake for 5 minutes, or until lightly golden.

3 Put the cream, butter, honey and sugar in a saucepan and stir over
medium heat until the sugar has dissolved. Remove from the heat and
stir in the toasted nuts and figs. Spoon the mixture into the pastry case
and bake for 30 minutes. Remove and cool until firm before slicing.

Apple Turnovers

Makes 12

500 g (1 lb 2 oz) ready-made puff pastry
1 egg white, lightly beaten
caster (superfine) sugar, to sprinkle

FILLING
220 g (7³/4 oz/1 cup) tinned pie apple
1–2 tablespoons caster (superfine) sugar, to taste
40 g (1¹/2 oz/¹/3 cup) raisins, chopped
30 g (1 oz/¹/4 cup) walnuts, chopped

1   Preheat the oven to 210°C (415°F/Gas 6–7). Lightly grease a baking
    tray. Roll the pastry on a lightly floured surface to 45 x 35 cm
    (18 x 14 inches). Cut out twelve 10 cm (4 inch) rounds.

2   To make the apple filling, mix together the apple, sugar, raisins and
    walnuts. Divide the filling among the pastry rounds, then brush the
    edges with water. Fold in half and pinch firmly together to seal. Use
    the back of a knife to push up the pastry edge at intervals.

3   Brush the tops with egg white and sprinkle with caster sugar. Make
    two small slits in the top of each turnover. Bake for 15 minutes, then
    lower the oven temperature to 190°C (375°F/Gas 5) and bake for
    10 minutes, or until golden. Delicious served warm.

You can make equally delicious turnovers by
substituting the same quantity of cooked or
tinned pears or rhubarb for the apple.

Lemon Brulée Tarts

Makes 4

315 ml (10³/4 fl oz/1¹/4 cups) pouring (whipping) cream
2 teaspoons grated lemon zest
4 egg yolks
2 tablespoons caster (superfine) sugar
2 teaspoons cornflour (cornstarch)
2 tablespoons lemon juice
410 g (14¹/2 oz) ready-made puff pastry
90 g (3¹/4 oz/scant ¹/2 cup) sugar

1   Heat the cream in a saucepan with the lemon zest until almost boiling. Allow to cool slightly. Whisk the egg yolks, sugar, cornflour and lemon juice in a bowl until thick and pale.

2   Add the warm cream gradually, whisking constantly. Strain into a clean pan and stir over low heat until thickened slightly—the mixture should coat the back of a wooden spoon. Pour into a heatproof bowl, cover with plastic wrap and refrigerate for several hours or overnight.

3   Preheat the oven to 210°C (415°F/Gas 6–7). Lightly grease four 12 cm (4¹/2 inch) shallow loose-based flan (tart) tins. Roll out the pastry to 48 x 25 cm (19 x 10 inches), then cut four rounds, large enough to fit the base and side of the tart tins. Line each tin with pastry, trim the edges and prick the bases lightly with a fork. Line with baking paper and fill with baking beads, dried beans or uncooked rice. Bake for 15 minutes, discard the paper and beads and return to the oven for another 5 minutes, or until lightly golden. Leave to cool.

4 Spoon the lemon custard into each pastry case and smooth the top, leaving a little room for the sugar layer. Cover the edges of the pastry with foil and sprinkle the sugar generously over the surface of the custard in an even layer.

5 Cook under a preheated grill (broiler) until the sugar just begins to colour. Put the tarts close to the grill so they brown quickly, but watch carefully that they do not burn. Serve immediately.

Pumpkin Pie

Serves 6–8

155 g (5¹/2 oz/1¹/4 cups) plain (all-purpose) flour

100 g (3¹/2 oz) unsalted butter, chilled and cubed

2 teaspoons caster (superfine) sugar

4 tablespoons iced water

FILLING

2 eggs, lightly beaten

185 g (6¹/4 oz/1 cup) soft brown sugar

750 g (1 lb 10 oz) butternut pumpkin (squash), cubed, boiled and
   mashed, then pushed through a sieve and cooled

80 ml (2¹/2 fl oz/¹/3 cup) pouring (whipping) cream

1 tablespoon sweet sherry or brandy

¹/2 teaspoon ground ginger

¹/2 teaspoon ground nutmeg

1 teaspoon ground cinnamon

1 Sift the flour into a bowl and rub in the butter, using your fingertips, until the mixture resembles breadcrumbs. Mix in the sugar. Make a well in the centre, add almost all the iced water and mix with a flat-bladed knife, using a cutting action, until the mixture comes together in beads—add more iced water if needed. Gather the dough and put on a lightly floured surface. Press into a ball and flatten slightly. Cover in plastic wrap and refrigerate for 20 minutes.

2 Roll out the pastry between two sheets of baking paper large enough to cover the base and side of a 23 x 18 x 3 cm (9 x 7 x 1¹/4 inch) pie dish. Line the dish with pastry, trim the excess and crimp the edges with a fork. Cover with plastic wrap and refrigerate for 20 minutes.

3 Preheat the oven to 180°C (350°F/Gas 4). Line the pastry case with crumpled baking paper and fill with baking beads, dried beans or uncooked rice. Bake for 10 minutes, then remove the paper and beads. Bake for another 10 minutes, or until lightly golden. Cool.

4 To make the filling, whisk the eggs and sugar in a bowl. Stir in the cooled pumpkin, cream, sherry and the spices. Pour into the pastry case and bake for 1 hour, or until set—cover the edges with foil if browning too quickly. Cool before serving.

Summer Berry Tart

Serves 4–6

125 g (4¹/2 oz/1 cup) plain (all-purpose) flour
90 g (3¹/4 oz) unsalted butter, chilled and cubed
2 tablespoons icing (confectioners') sugar
1–2 tablespoons iced water

FILLING

3 egg yolks
2 tablespoons caster (superfine) sugar
2 tablespoons cornflour (cornstarch)
250 ml (9 fl oz/1 cup) milk
1 teaspoon natural vanilla extract
250 g (9 oz/1²/3 cups) fresh strawberries, halved
125 g (4¹/2 oz/³/4 cup) fresh blueberries
125 g (4¹/2 oz/1 cup) fresh raspberries
1–2 tablespoons baby apple gel

1 Preheat the oven to 180°C (350°F/Gas 4). Lightly grease a 20 cm
   (8 inch) round, loose-based, fluted flan (tart) tin. Sift the flour into a
   bowl and rub in the butter, using your fingertips, until the mixture
   resembles fine breadcrumbs. Mix in the sugar. Make a well in the
   centre and add almost all the iced water. Mix with a flat-bladed knife,
   using a cutting action, until the mixture comes together in beads,
   adding more iced water if the dough is too dry.

2 Roll out the pastry between two sheets of baking paper to fit the
   base and side of the tart tin. Line the tin with the pastry and trim
   away any excess. Refrigerate for 20 minutes. Line the tin with
   baking paper and fill with baking beads, dried beans or uncooked rice.

Bake for 15 minutes, then remove the paper and beads. Bake the pastry for another 15 minutes, or until golden.

3   To make the filling, place the egg yolks, sugar and cornflour in a bowl and whisk until pale. Heat the milk in a small saucepan until almost boiling, then remove from the heat and add gradually to the egg mixture, beating constantly. Strain back into the pan. Stir constantly over low heat for 3 minutes, or until the mixture boils and thickens. Remove from the heat and add the vanilla extract. Transfer to a bowl, cover with plastic wrap and set aside to cool.

4   Spread the filling in the pastry case and top with the berries. Heat the apple gel in a heatproof bowl in a saucepan of simmering water, or in the microwave, until it becomes liquid. Brush over the fruit with a pastry brush. Allow to set before cutting.

Passionfruit and Mango Millefeuille

Serves 4

PASSIONFRUIT CURD
3 eggs
60 g (2 1/4 oz) unsalted butter
125 g (4 1/2 oz/1/2 cup) passionfruit pulp
125 g (4 1/2 oz/heaped 1/2 cup) sugar

500 g (1 lb 2 oz) ready-made puff pastry
300 ml (10 1/2 fl oz/1 1/4 cups) pouring (whipping) cream
2 tablespoons icing (confectioners') sugar
1 teaspoon natural vanilla extract
1 large ripe mango, thinly sliced
sifted icing (confectioners') sugar, extra, to sprinkle

1 To make the passionfruit curd, beat the eggs well, then strain into a heatproof bowl and stir in the remaining ingredients. Place the bowl over a saucepan of simmering water and stir with a wooden spoon for 15–20 minutes, or until the butter has melted and the mixture has thickened slightly and coats the back of the spoon. Cool, then transfer to a bowl, cover with plastic wrap and chill until required.

2 Preheat the oven to 200°C (400°F/Gas 6). Line a large baking tray with baking paper. Roll the pastry to a 30 x 35 cm (12 x 14 inch) rectangle and transfer to the tray. Cover and refrigerate for 20 minutes. Sprinkle lightly with water and prick all over with a fork. Bake for 25 minutes, or until puffed and golden. Cool completely on a wire rack.

3 Whisk the cream with the icing sugar and vanilla extract until firm peaks form. Carefully trim the pastry sheet and cut into three even-sized strips lengthways. Spread one layer of pastry with half the passionfruit curd, spreading evenly and to the edges. Top this with half the whipped cream and then top with half the mango flesh. Place a second sheet of pastry on top and repeat the process. Top with the remaining pastry sheet and sprinkle liberally with icing sugar. Carefully transfer to a serving plate. Use a serrated knife to cut into slices.

 Instead of making one long millefeuille, you might prefer to make four individual ones.

index